GP cloth 7⁵⁰

The Diary of

Latoya

Hunter

꒜ ꒜ ꒜

The Diary of Latoya Hunter

My First Year in Junior High

by

Latoya Hunter

↊ ↊ ↊

CROWN PUBLISHERS, INC.

NEW YORK

Published by Crown Publishers, Inc., 201 East 50th Street, New York, New York 10022. Member of the Crown Publishing Group.

CROWN is a trademark of Crown Publishers, Inc.

Manufactured in the United States of America

Library of Congress Cataloging-in-Publication Data

Hunter, Latoya.
The diary of Latoya Hunter.—1st ed.
    Summary: Presents the diary of twelve-year-old Latoya Hunter as she goes through her first year of junior high school in the Bronx.
    1. Hunter, Latoya—Diaries—Juvenile literature.   2. Children of immigrants—New York (N.Y.)—Diaries—Juvenile literature.   3. West Indian Americans—New York (N.Y.)—Diaries—Juvenile literature.   4. Children's writings, American—New York (N.Y.)   5. Education, Elementary—New York (N.Y.)—Juvenile literature.   6. Bronx (New York, N.Y.)—Biography—Juvenile literature.   7. New York (N.Y.)—Biography—Juvenile literature.   [1. Hunter, Latoya.   2. West Indian Americans—Biography.   3. Bronx (New York, N.Y.)—Biography.   4. Schools.   5. Diaries.   6. Children's writings.]   I. Title.
F128.9.W54H86   1992
974.7'1043'092—dc20
[B]   92-8384
                                                                                      CIP
                                                                                       AC

ISBN 0-517-58511-1

10   9   8   7   6   5   4   3   2

I dedicate this book to my family: Linneth, Linton, Rondah, Clifton, Anthony, and to the new additions: Devoy, Kevaughn, and Michelle. I would also like to dedicate this book to all my relatives in Canada and Jamaica, especially my grandparents. Thank you all for your support. And to Mr. Robert Pelka, thank you for believing in me.

Editor's Note

The origin of this book stems from a *New York Times* article describing the graduation of the sixth-grade class from P.S. 94 in the Bronx. The class had several exceptional students, but its teacher, Robert Pelka, singled out Latoya Hunter for her "incredible writing talent." On her final report card, he wrote simply, "The world is waiting for Latoya!"

I contacted Mr. Pelka and asked if he thought Latoya would like to keep a diary of her first year in junior high. He talked to his pupil and wrote back that she and her parents would be interested in meeting with me. An appointment was made; I arrived, accompanied by my twenty-three-year-old assistant, Laura Hildebrand, who would, I thought, have a much closer rapport with Latoya than I. (This turned out to be true, as you'll see when you read the diary.)

Latoya was shy but self-possessed, obviously smart and equally obviously excited by the prospect of the diary. We commissioned two-weeks' worth of work. She sent them, and we loved them; we signed a contract for the whole book. The diary was born.

Every word in this diary is Latoya's. We have, occasionally, corrected syntax and spelling when they seemed mistakes of speed. The mistakes of vernacular, we've left alone. Keeping a diary over a ten-month span is arduous work even for a grown-up, and there were days when

Latoya's entries were obviously written more out of duty than passion. In some cases, I've left them as is, in others I've asked Latoya to expand and amplify. In that sense, and because, of course, Latoya knew she was writing for publication, this is not a "pure" work. Yet it seems to me remarkably honest nevertheless, and unquestionably it reveals the soul of an extraordinary young girl whom all of us who have worked with her have come to love.

RICHARD MAREK

The Diary of

Latoya

Hunter

℮ ℮ ℮

─────── ✍ ✍ ✍ ───────

September 10, 1990

Dear Diary,

It is hard to believe that this is the day I have anticipated and looked forward to for such a long time. The sun still rose in the East and set again in the West, the crisis in Iraq is still going strong and Oprah Winfrey still preached at 4:00 about other people's business. This may sound funny but somewhere in the back of my mind I thought the world would stop for my first day of JH. The day proved me wrong and I've grown to realize that nothing will be quite as I dreamed them up.

My teachers are one of my biggest disappointments. In this crazy dream world of mine my teachers were cool and calm and bright and welcoming. They were really just normal people making their livings. Ms. Johnson is the science teacher. She is Australian-Chinese. I have never met a teacher who gave so many rules. Her rules for the year took up at least 3 pages of my notebook. All my other teachers are just average. They aren't, or don't seem to be nothing above or under that. Maybe during the year they'll prove to be above, or hopefully not under. My other courses are math, English, French, social studies, and Home and Careers. There are none I'm really excited about.

Diary, there isn't much of a welcoming committee at this school. However, there's a day 8th & 9th graders set out to show freshmen how they feel about us. They call it Freshman Day. It may sound sweet but it's not at all. What they set out to do is terrorize us. They really seem to want to hurt us. It's a tradition I guess. I hope with God's help that I'll be able to make it through without any broken bones.

Well, today I think I could say J.H.S. is almost like an earthly version of hell.

September 11, 1990

Dear Diary,

I never thought I'd get desperate enough to say this but I envy you. You don't have to live in this troubled world; all you do is hear about it. You don't have to go to J.H. and watch the clock, praying for dismissal time to come. You also don't have to go through a situation like sitting in a cafeteria watching others laughing and talking and you don't know anyone. To sit there and eat the food that is just terrible because there's nothing else to do.

You don't do any of those things. All you do is listen to pathetic twelve-year-olds like me tell you about it.

I guess you can tell how my day went. Diary, what am I going to do? My best friend left to go to another school. I wish she could be with me. We had so much fun together. She moved right before summer started. She doesn't live anywhere close so it would be much easier if she stayed at the school closest to her. That's the only part of it that's easy. The hardest part is not being together.

September 12, 1990

Dear Diary,

The dreaded Freshman Day is drawing near. I can see into the deranged minds of the 8th & 9th graders. They can't wait. I've heard rumors that they attack kids in the hall. I wonder if that could be true. Are they that cruel? I feel there will be a lot of fights between freshmen and seniors, I hope I won't be in any of them. The thing is, I know the kind of people they'll be aiming for. They are the quiet ones, the ones who aren't into the crowd, the kids who don't act like animals on the street. That's the kind of person I am. That's just how I am and how I'll leave J.H.S. 80. I'm not about to change to fit in their dead-in-an-alley-headed crowd. I intend to make something of myself. Life is too precious to waste.

September 13, 1990

Dear Diary,

Is it strange for someone to *want* to get sick so they can't leave their house for a day? Well, I do and you know why—it's Freshman's Day eve and tis not the season to be jolly. The older kids are really trying to make us believe like we're trespassing on their property. Well, it isn't theirs alone.

3

If there is a special diary way of praying, pray I'll come home in one piece. I'll write to you tomorrow. If I survive.

September 14, 1990

Dear Diary,

I can't believe I'm here writing to you with no scratches or bruises. I actually made it! Something must have snapped in the minds of the older kids. Maybe they remembered when they were freshmen themselves because there were only a few fights today. I witnessed one of them with a geeky looking boy who really fought back, badly as he did. They didn't really bother girls. I think that was decent of them. I'm really relieved as you may guess.

In the morning, Mr. Gluck, the principal announced that if anyone even thought of touching us it would mean suspension. Maybe that was why this Freshman Day was so much calmer. Whatever reason why, I appreciate it.

Well Diary, what I assume was the worst week of J.H. is over. I hope things will get better next week. It has to. It can't get any worse . . . or can it?

September 16, 1990

Dear Diary,

This weekend was the best I've had for a long time. On Saturday I went to a party all the way in Brooklyn. My parents wouldn't normally let me go so far just for a party, especially since they wouldn't be there but it was a cousin's party, so they made an exception. I don't think they wanted to go because it was only younger people like 25 & under.

It was a wonderful feeling not having them anywhere close. I felt independent. They always want to keep me in the house. I don't know all their motives, but I know protection is a big part. They don't realize that keeping me locked up just means that when I do go out there I'll be unprepared. I believe I need experience more than anything to get along in N.Y.C. I live in the Bronx. I'd much rather live in Manhattan because it's what I pictured New York to be in Jamaica with its big buildings and city-like sights. I live on a street where everything seems so ugly to me. The sidewalks, the houses, even my own house. From the outside it looks really broken down. It needs everything done to it to improve it. The inside is really small. It has three bedrooms, the smallest one, mine. I can hardly move around in it. I would say it's the best the family could do right now, but I don't believe it. I'm sure there's a better place out there for us it's just no one seems to be looking for it right now.

Most people don't understand how I think. I have so many ideas that don't check in other people's minds. My parents are the main people who can't see into them. I would like to please my parents and let go of my ideas but I can't. They're stuck in my mind. Like at this party, there were a lot of guys. I like guys. There, I said it. It's easy to say it to you, but my mother would give me a real hard time if she heard me say that. She believes a normal twelve-year-old should only obey her parents, go to school, learn her lessons, and come home everyday and listen to her parents some more. There is no such thing as a person like that! If I like a boy, she could talk and talk but it can't stop me from liking him.

At the party, a guy tried to talk to me and I gave him a wrong number to call. He was *ugly*, his breath stank, it was horrible. I may sound stuck up, but in this case I'll risk it. He was a dog! I had a good time anyway. My cousin dropped me home at 5:00 in the morning! It lasted longer than I thought.

Anyhow, I stayed home from church. I was too tired! I chilled out inside all day. I watched a lot of t.v., which is one of the only things I'm good at. My parents are cool with me watching t.v., at least it keeps me off the streets.

September 17, 1990

Dear Diary,

I have good news. On Thursday and Friday there'll be no school. It's the Jewish New Year. It doesn't count for me because I'm not Jewish. I really respect these people though. Last year in school I learned about Adolph Hitler and all the terrible things he did to them. He was a psycho if you ask me. I can't understand why people discriminate against others for simple things like skin color and religion. I strongly believe this world should be non-racist. I've never come across discrimination against me for me being black. I know racism is going on in all parts of the world but the fight is still going on too. That is something to be thankful for. Things like Mandela recently being freed has kept my hope alive.

September 18, 1990

Dear Diary,

Today felt like a sneak preview of winter and a sad end to summer. It was fun while it lasted. I spent most of August in Toronto. It's such a beautiful city. It's clean and peaceful. In other words, not my style. I like action. It's not so much the place that appeals to me, it's my relatives living there. That includes my grandparents on my mom's side, my aunt Chunnie, and four of my cousins. The oldest is 20 and the youngest is now 16. That's the only girl, Ann. We grew up like sisters! Like me their mom lived apart from them (in Canada), then took them up. Then she took up my grandparents. My cousins are who I grew up with excluding my Aunt Chunnie and her youngest son, and they were the only people I knew how to love until I was eight. That's when I left Jamaica, my homeland, the place where my life was crafted. Sadly, until that time, my life was crafted without my parents. They were here in N.Y., struggling to make enough money to get my sister, two brothers and me to share with them the American dream. I didn't know my father until he met us at the airport. He left when I was a baby. I've really gotten to know him over the past four years though. When I first saw him at the airport, I thought "Well this is the famous Daddy!" Everyone, even my cousins call him Daddy. Our families were that close. I can't forget he was in a hurry to get home to watch a big baseball game on t.v. After that was over, he pretty much put all his attention into us. I can remember once when I was sick, and I'll never forget this, he made me soup and made me stay in bed. I was like, "Wow! This is like t.v." I guess in Jamaica I never pictured a father making soup for his kid. I pictured the mother doing those things, never the man. He isn't easily upset or worked up. He hardly yells at me. That works with me because if I do something wrong and someone yells at me, I don't feel guilty about what I've done, just angry at the person yelling. He just goes with the flow. He was really easy to get used to.

My mother is really complex though. I still don't understand her. I had a faint memory of her while I was in Jamaica. She had left when I was 3 or 4. Anyways, they succeeded in getting my brothers, sister and myself up here. When we first got here she worked as a live-in housekeeper in Poughkeepsie for some very rich people. She only came home on Friday and left again on Sunday. We hardly ever saw her but she called all the time. What got her to quit was when I first started going to P.S. 94. I was in computer class for the first time and when I saw that everyone knew what to do, I got depressed. I never saw one before in my life. I cried and cried and the teacher sent me home because I said I had a stomach ache.

Anyway, my mom heard about it and decided she didn't want to be away when things like that happened. I finally had her full-time. We enjoyed ourselves at first, being together all the time. But the excitement wore off and when I was around ten, we began the phase we're in now.

As I said, I'm living in the Bronx, a place where walking alone at night is a major risk. The streets are so dirty and there's graffiti everywhere. It really makes you feel down to walk around and see the things around you. The only colors I see are brown and grey—dull colors. Maybe there are others but the dull ones are the ones I see. Maybe if the streets were cleaner, and I would see colors like red and yellow, my surroundings would be more appealing but for now, all I see is dullness and cloudiness. There aren't any pleasant smells coming from anywhere as I walk the neighborhood—just the smell of nothingness. There are a few stores very close to where I live. They are one of the few things that are familiar to me in this neighborhood. Everyone knows me in these stores because if nothing else, I'm a junk food fanatic! There's one at the corner, one around the corner and one in between. Besides them, everything is grey.

Am I lucky or what? I would say not but it wouldn't be true entirely. There are so many opportunities we've gotten that we wouldn't dream of getting in Jamaica. I guess that's why they call this the land of opportunity. My mom works in a hospital not far from our house. She's a nurses assistant, my father does security work. It isn't a big income family but I'll make it. I think we all will.

September 19, 1990

Dear Diary,

Just knowing I don't have to go to school tomorrow made my entire day today. I stayed outside with my friends after school. I haven't done that for such a long time. I almost forgot how much fun I had with them.

I'll tell you about Deborah first, she's a distant cousin. She's the one who showed me around at first and introduced me to people. She's like the leader of our crew. She can act pushy sometimes but I like her. We would call her a Don

Girl in Jamaican. That means she's someone you just respect.

Then there's Denise and Monique, they're sisters, but they don't really get along. Denise changes her personality a lot and frankly I can't keep up with her. Monique however, stays the same. She's funny and just a fun-loving person. There's also Lisa and Isabelle. Lisa's cool, Isabelle's someone I can't explain. I'm not really crazy about her.

They, especially Deborah, have taught me a lot. Over the years they've shown me how to come out of my shell and have fun. They were the ones who introduced me to things like parties, music, boys . . . some crazy things we've done! One time we planned to go visit a cemetery at night. Is that crazy or what? Only we would do something like that!

September 20, 1990

Dear Diary,

I spent the day helping out my friend Anika. She's moving out of her apartment. I'll still get to see her though, she's still going to go to my school.

We met an old lady on the street. We walked with her to the bus stop. I think in that short time we spent walking, she actually told us her life story. She told us she's going back to high school and she seemed to be proud of herself. She told us about God and that He had been her best friend ever since she was our age. It was really interesting to listen to someone who has lived and experienced so much. At first, I was just trying not to be rude so I listened, but soon I found myself wanting to hear what she had to say. I realize now that everyone has a life to them. I see so many faces everyday, it was nice to go beyond the face for once.

September 21, 1990

Dear Diary,

Today three of my relatives from Canada came for a visit; my grandfather and two boy cousins Glendon and Dexton. They'll be here until Sunday. I hope God keeps them safe for the few days they'll be here. The other day a guy from Utah was stabbed to death while protecting his family on the train. That is a sad example of the crime in New York especially since he was just visiting for the weekend. The crime is really getting ridiculous here.

If I had a choice now, I would choose to leave this place. I just can't feel safe here. I have good reasons too. My father was almost shot when he used to drive a cab at nights. My brother also came close to being a victim of crime. He was held up at gunpoint at the movie theater where he works in Manhattan. Fortunately he wasn't hurt. I'm really scared to be here.

My friend Lisa wasn't as lucky with brothers as I was. Her

brother was shot 12 times just the other day. I heard he was on the way to the store and someone waited for him and did the job. It was probably drug-related. He looked like someone involved in those things, sorry to say. She's still mourning his death. Anyways Diary, that's the way things are in New York city, my home.

September 23, 1990

Dear Diary,

The weekend was great as always. On Saturday I went to see my aunt Rita. She lives 15 minutes away in the Bronx. Everyone went: my parents, sister, and my relatives visiting from Canada. It was a nice evening. Afterwards I went to my friend's sister's baby shower. I couldn't stay long though because I wasn't supposed to be there in the first place. My mother disapproves of me being at that house. I don't know what she thinks goes on up there but I know she's wrong. She wrong about everything. She thinks there are things going on that she doesn't know about, but there aren't. I think in her mind she sees Deborah and everyone else with a bunch of guys partying and making out—what else could she think? I think she knows I wouldn't do anything like drugs. If only she'd understand, then I wouldn't feel guilty every time I want to be with my friends.

Today, Sunday, I went to church. My relatives left and

went back home. It was nice having them here, even for a short time. I get to take communion now. Personally I don't like the bread but it's suppose to be the body of Christ so I eat it. I always make sure however that I have candy to get the taste out of my mouth. Well Diary, the vacation is over. I have to face school tomorrow. I don't mind though, I'm going to try to feel comfortable there—I'll really like my classes, and make more friends. I think things would really look up then. So far I like Home and Careers. I'm not so crazy about the teacher but I like the idea of planning and thinking about later on in life.

September 25, 1990

Dear Diary,

Why does school have to come with music teachers?! You would not believe what mine is going to make the class do. I'm talking major embarrassing! The whole class has to sing "We Are the World" in front of the whole school! Can you believe it? I mean, the song is so old. It's not fair! I bet the kids will boo us off the stage, they're good at that if anything. We're supposed to do this thing on Wednesday. Talk about short notice! We rehearsed and I must say, sound terrible. The boys are off key and it's just a mess. I hope we get it together before Wednesday, we can't afford to give the older kids more reason not to like us.

September 30, 1990

Dear Diary,

I think I need a name for you. You've become like a best friend to me, you're someone I can talk to without being argued with. I think I know just the name for you. I'll call you Janice after my best friend from Jamaica. We were like sisters before I left. Over the years we've grown apart though, the letters have stopped but that friendship is still going on within me!

So today I christen you diary, Janice Page.

October 1, 1990

Dear Janice,

Something horrible happened today. I was walking to the store when suddenly a gray car pulled up beside me. There was a middle-aged Puerto-rican man with a terrible looking beard inside. He blew his horn and called me to come inside, he was holding up money which was supposed to be a lure. It was so frightening. I kept on walking and tried my best to ignore him. I turned into the store and when I came outside he was gone.

I can't help but wonder about if another girl who wasn't as cautious as me decided to go to that terrible man. What would he do to her? Why did the world have to come with people who have to hurt other people not only physically but mentally, in order to please themselves? As I am writing this, that man might have succeeded in his quest. If he had attacked me I don't know what I'd do. I would of course panic. I'm a panicky person, but I think since I'm not physical, I'd try to talk him out of his plan. I couldn't attack him or try to fight him, that definitely wouldn't work. I'm not very strong. I feel sorry for his victim and believe it or not, my sympathy goes out to him too. Someone who could do something as terrible as take away children and do whatever they feel to them and emotionally scar the lives of his victim and their loved ones, deserves not only hate but also pity.

I'm going to try to sleep now, but it'll be hard knowing that man and many of his kind are out there somewhere.

October 2, 1990

Dear Janice,

I t's hard to believe but people change as rapidly as the world does. If I had kept you as a diary two years ago, you would have heard about Jimmy. He was the first guy who I was close to and who was a real friend to me. I liked him because other boys always seemed to be in a popularity contest, and he didn't care about that stuff. He was handsome and everything but he never let it get to his

head. Well lately he's been going to the other side. He has
a new walk, new talk, new look—the works! He ignores me,
I guess I'm not popular enough for him! He just isn't the
same.

October 3, 1990

Dear Janice,

Some people just weren't made for certain professions.
My computer teacher proved that today. Kids are
supposed to go to school to learn new things, vocabulary
is one of them, but the words this teacher used! Parents
don't send their kids to school to learn obscenities.
Maybe she just had a bad case of P.M.S. but that still
doesn't give her the right to say those words. What are
we students suppose to go home and say, "Listen mom
I learned a new word!" It's not right. If she wants us to
respect her she has to respect us first. Some kids in my
class talked to our homeroom teacher Mr. Sontze about
it. As usual he can't do anything. I don't think we want
to go to the principal. If it gets worse, maybe.

October 5, 1990

Dear Janice,

Today in gym class we watched a video on how girls should protect themselves from rape. These subjects are ones we would never even discuss in public school. Well, that isn't exactly true—my ex-teacher Mr. Pelka always made sure his students were aware of things like that. He really cared about us and we cared back. I should tell you more about him someday, but I don't want to get off the subject like I almost always do. We watched the video and I found it hard to believe just how sleazy some men could be. It gave me joy to see the ladies hurt each one of them. Their techniques were really good but I'm not athletic enough to carry out any of them. It's funny, but in Jamaica I wasn't even aware of crime. Maybe it's because I was young or maybe it's because I came from such a rural area, but it just wasn't a problem. I'd love to have that state of mind again. I just hope I'm never in a crime situation like my father and brother were in.

October 6, 1990

Dear Janice,

Today my friend Isabelle had a fit in her house. It was because of her mother. She's never home and she expects Isabelle to stay by herself. Today she was extra late because she was out with her boyfriend. Isabelle was really mad. She called her father and told him she wanted to live with him because her mother only cared about one person— her boyfriend. She was so upset. She was throwing things all over the place and crying. I never saw her like that before. It was really sad to see. I felt bad when I had to leave her all by herself. I hope she and her mother work it out but all mothers are the same. They think that you're young and shouldn't have an opinion. It's really hard to communicate with my parents. They'll listen to me but that's about it. They hardly take me seriously and it's because of my age. It's like discrimination! If you do speak your mind, you end up getting beaten. The real pain doesn't come from the belt though, it comes from inside. That's the worst pain you could ever feel.

———— ✄ ✄ ✄ ————

October 7, 1990

Dear Janice,

This weekend was spent at home, at my brother's house and at church. My brothers just moved out recently. They don't live very far though, about 15 minutes away from the house. Their new house is nice. I like it there. They're both so funny. One is Dave and the other is Courtney. They're like twins except they look nothing alike and are a couple years apart. Dave is 23 and Courtney is 25. We don't communicate much anymore—they've got girlfriends and they're making new lives for themselves. It's impossible now to have a close relationship with either of them.

After church today I felt the urge to do something independent. I started walking and found myself heading home. Church and home aren't too close together so when I did get home I got in trouble with both parents—it's usually only my mom, but my father didn't approve either. That's really embarrassing that they got upset for that! I thought I was more grown than that. I know I am, but they don't. This whole entry is embarrassing. I'm not a baby, I can't believe they think that way of me. I only wanted to prove I could do something by myself. Even that is a crime these days in the parents law book. I can't do anything right these days.

October 8, 1990

Dear Janice,

Today I saw my old teacher, I was talking about the other day. I thought this should be the day I tell you about him. His name is Robert Pelka. He's a heavy man but that only means there's more of him to love. There's just something about him that makes him impossible not to like. He's warm, caring, loving and everything else that comes with a great human being. He didn't only teach me academic things like math, English and so on. He taught me how to be open-minded to all kinds of people. He did that by making us empathize with other people, in other words, put ourselves in their place and write about it. I went from being a sister of retarded boy named Victor to being a Jewish girl whose family was taken away from me back in the Hitler days.

Mr. Pelka made things we'd normally learn about from history books sort of come alive, it's like you're there. Those are just some of the things he introduced me to. The things he changed about me are innumerable. The world should know this man. He probably won't go down in any major history books but if this diary counts as a book of history, he just did.

October 9, 1990,

Dear Janice,

I can't believe it! I got a 95 on my math test. That's really good considering I'm taking a ninth grade math course. 9th grade math isn't that hard, you just have to know certain things before you can solve a problem. That's about all that happened today. My life is so boring sometimes! I'm so grateful for the little t.v. in my room. I don't know how people ever lived without it. It's scary just thinking about it. When I'm stuck inside, it sort of brings me outside to the world. These walls of my room, so close together, form such a small room. I try to brighten it up because when the T.V. is off, there's nothing else to do but stare at everything and think. I have a big collection of teddy bears. I can only remember where two or three of them came from and some how the rest ended up sitting in my room. I don't play with them, I just look at them. On the wall above my bed I have what seems to be thousands of posters of my favorite singers. Most of them are guys, so my mother has a problem with them. My room just wouldn't be complete without them, but if the day ever came where I had to get rid of them, I'd have to leave the one of Big Daddy Kane. He's this really sexy rapper that makes my knees go weak when I see him. His poster is larger than all the rest and he has a wall for himself. I wouldn't change anything in it, but I would change the room itself!

Someday I hope to even write a movie myself. It'll be

really successful and all my favorite actors and actresses will be in it. I'll be another Jackie Collins but better. Well a girl can dream, that's the easy but it's making it become a reality—that's the hard part.

October 10, 1990

Dear Janice,

I didn't tell you this before but I have a little niece or nephew on the way. I can be thankful to my sister Rondah for that. I never had a younger sister or brother so I guess this is as close as I'll get to one. I can't wait to have a baby in the house and it's for the same reason most kids my age would not want one. Because it will take attention away from me. I hate attention! If something good happens and I was the reason for it everyone starts paying attention to me and are so nice to me. It's sickening when people, for no real reason, come up to my room when it's something they wouldn't ordinarily do. Over the years when I didn't get any attention I got used to being alone and I like it. I just don't need anyone around me. I've found I'm much happier sitting in my room watching t.v. by myself. That means no arguments and no pressuring. To understand this entry you'd have to live my life for at least a day. In the morning don't do anything special. See the treatment you get. In the afternoon do something that could mean lots of things to everyone involved. After that, in the evening, compare the treatment you now get to what you got earlier, before your little deed. I think you'll see the difference and the reason I feel this way.

Since no one could ever live my life for even a short time, just look at it this way. Pretend you're a boy trying to get the attention of a certain girl. She's shown no interest in you until you purchased a really hot car. To be seen in one of those would mean everything to her. All of a sudden after you buy the car she's all over you. You can't help but wonder if it's you she loves or the car. It's not that I think I'm loved only for things I do. It's just that I get good grades and I think that if I had a learning disability I wouldn't be accepted the same. I think what my mother enjoys most is bragging about me to friends and if she didn't have that, I don't think she would really appreciate me. When I got the chance to do this diary for publication, she didn't display much to me. She never actually said, "I'm proud of you!" She never told me how she felt. All I know is since I began to write this diary I've been getting a lot more attention from her. Sometimes I feel it's so fake, sometimes I think really negative. I want to be appreciated for me—good grades or no good grades.

October 11, 1990

Dear Janice,

I talked to Isabelle today. Remember she had that problem with her mother? Well, she finally worked up the nerve to talk to her mother and what do you know? She's grounded. Just because she gave her opinion. Isabelle's really frustrated now. I could understand why. I've told you that most of my opinions don't check with my parents. If I had a problem I don't even think I'd talk to them about it. They'd just say, "When I was your age I could never walk up to my mother and tell her anything like that. I'd just get smacked over." When I try to say, "That was your day and maybe since this is a new day there should be a new way," I just get what they would get from their mother. What can I say? Parents just don't understand. It's no use to try to make them. It'll just backfire on you. Most kids would give up on trying to get understanding on both their parent's side, but not me. I'm a very stubborn girl. I explain my case from all sides. I try every trick in the book just to get approval on an issue.

October 12, 1990

Dear Janice,

Today after school I went to my brother's house. I had fun as usual. I played dominos with Rondah, Dave's girl-friend Sandra, and I brought along my friend/cousin Deborah. I'm not really good at dominos but I got through o.k. Us Jamaicans love dominos—the men do anyway. At family gatherings the women talk and dance and the men sit around a table of dominos. Once there, they don't want to get up.

Anyways, I enjoyed the evening a lot. We listened to Jamaican music (my favorite kind) until it was time to go home. Since my brothers moved out we've been doing these things like every three weeks. They feel good, I think to be able to do whatever they want in their own house where they're boss. Entertaining is one thing they can do anytime they want now so I suppose they're taking advantage of it.

October 15, 1990

Dear Janice,

I went to the movies this weekend. I saw "Ghost" and "Avalon." "Ghost" was pretty good. It had a great cast—Patrick Swayze, Demi Moore and Whoopie Goldberg. It was a really romantic film. I go for that mushy stuff. I cried over the last episode of Family Ties. That's just the way I am.

Unlike "Ghost," "Avalon" wasn't all that good. It was so long and it had no point to it. It just seemed to go on and on and on. Rondah and I were the first ones out of the movie theater. It was torture to sit through that movie—it's not good for entertaining, only for putting someone to sleep. I give it two thumbs down and right now, I should put my pen down until tomorrow.

October 16, 1990

Dear Janice,

Today Rondah asked me if her suspicions of an upcoming shower were true. I lied like a pro. I had her convinced. I looked her straight in the eye and I didn't even laugh. I should lie more often—just kidding. Anyway, I'm really excited about the baby. Even though Rondah'll be a single mom, I think we'll pull through. She's a really strong individual. She can do anything if she puts her mind to it. I don't think about the father much he's never around and I bet that's the way it will be when the baby comes. He isn't the fatherly type.

Rondah says she wants the whole Hunter clan to take a trip to Jamaica in Easter. You don't have any idea how much I want to pack up and go back but—not to live. If I was to live there again I'd live in Kingston. I think it's the most advanced spot on the whole island. Where I lived in St. Ann, there was only one channel received on all the televisions in the Parish. Can you imagine? I honestly don't know how I lived like that. What I miss most is being able to walk barefoot freely. Living with animals, from chickens to goats, seems amazing to me now. I kind of miss it.

Hopefully in Easter, I'll go back and relive a part of the life I've lost.

———— ❧ ❧ ❧ ————

October 17, 1990

Dear Janice,

Nothing seemed to go right today. I got up feeling low and am about to go to bed feeling low. The English teacher gave the class a 3 on the section sheet (that's a sheet of paper the class brings around all day and each teacher rates us from a 5 to a 0). Well, the homeroom teacher doesn't like anything under a 5 so we got detention. I had to walk home all by myself because by the time I came out, my friends had gone home. I came home to a messy room and accompanying me was tons of homework. I have a science test tomorrow on cells in both animals and plants. I have science 7th period so I guess I could get some studying in over the first six periods. I'll write to you tomorrow Janice. Wish me luck on the test!

October 18, 1990

Dear Janice,

I feel so sick! I wanted the stupid guidance counselor to send me home today but she said I wasn't sick enough. What did she want me to do? Stretch out on the floor and say, "Look at the pretty birdie go?" I slept my way through S.S. and in Gym I had to leave suddenly because I wanted to throw up. I should have headed straight to the guidance counselor's office and thrown up right on her desk. By Science I was a wreck, but I managed through the test okay. It was easy! If I wasn't so messed up I would have gotten through with it in a breeze. I hope tomorrow I will feel better.

October 19, 1990

Dear Janice,

I felt better today. I got my test back and I got an 85. Not bad huh? I blame the 15 points lost on the guidance counselor. Gym was fun! I love playing basketball. Since I started J.H. I've been finding myself trying out new things. Sports were not exactly an interest of mine before. But since the gym teacher said a grade higher than a U comes with participation, I've had no choice. But now, if I had a choice I would play sports. The computer teacher has lightened up since I last wrote to you about her. I'm not saying that she's a totally new woman. 90% of the old her is still there. She let us play with the software today. We played "Trail to Oregon." The class was enjoying themselves and I was too. We thought the woman had gotten personality change over night. I was almost at Oregon when guess what? She pulled the plug! Can you believe it? I was almost there. My pen and your page will meet tomorrow.

October 22, 1990

Dear Janice,

I've made a decision. I Latoya Hunter am going on a diet. I don't think I'm really fat. I weigh 112, but my so called friend Deborah always bugs me that I'm short and fat—like a tree stump. How rude! My sister always teases me too. Like I wrote earlier, some people have no heart. I know I'm just an average looking person. I wish I was gorgeous like those superstar models but I just am not. Maybe over the years as I get older, I'll grow into a prettier phase. So, I'm going on a diet. I'm not sure how to go through with it. Last year, a boy in my class went on a diet, and brought SLIM FAST to school everyday. I do not honestly think I have to be so drastic. I'll just plain and simply eat less. My mother is always going on diet—not actually going on them but planning and buying supplements for them. After doing all that, she says, "I'll start tomorrow." When tomorrow comes, she says "Tomorrow, I'll definitely start tomorrow." Then when her conscience does a job on her she'll drink a glass of the SLIM FAST or whatever and eat just the same amount of food she'd regularly eat. It's pitiful. I think she should just be satisfied the way she is—and no—I don't want to take my own advice! Hasta manana. (My ex-Spanish teacher would be proud.)

October 24, 1990

Dear Janice,

I have very exciting news. My brother Courtney is getting married! He called the family together today and told us. His fiancee Michelle is really nice, she says she'll make me a bridesmaid. I've always wanted to take part in a wedding and I've always wanted my brothers to find themselves girls they could love and trust. My other brother Dave has been with the same girl for over two years. They still haven't made the move to tie the knot but at least they've got love. Courtney is the oldest so I would suppose the ability to make a commitment comes with age. I'm just happy one of them is going to become a husband. Rondah's boyfriend is really flaky. I wouldn't want her to settle down with him. Even though he's the father of her child, he shouldn't be the one to spend her life with. I want for her and for me, someone who will always be there for us no matter what!

October 26, 1990

Dear Janice,

T.G.I.F. (Thank Goodness It's Friday). No more school for 2 days but I do have to do a report for Home & Careers. I have to choose a career and write about why it is important, etc. My first choice is journalism. I wouldn't mind working as a journalist at a newspaper—it's a steady job and I'd get to do my favorite thing which is writing. My second choice is psychology. I want to be a writer but maybe on the side I could be a mindhealer. I'll get ideas from my patients and write stories about them. I could see it now—people suing me because they think my latest novel was about the confidential information they told me when they were my patients! I know just how to avoid it, I'll use a different name for each occupation. Is that a criminal act? If it is I won't go through with it. I also have a dream of driving a bulldozier. It just appeals to me. I know it's strange but there are some things that have no explanation!

October 29, 1990

Dear Janice,

It's Monday again. School was okay. The class has detention tomorrow. We got a three in English again. I think I know why the class is always messing up in English. The teacher's too soft. She gives us easy work, things we've known for years. My idea of English class is that it should be more along the lines of a college course, not junior high. I want to go deeper into literature and study characters and examine what makes them tick. There is no challenge to her class. We tell her over and over again we want to learn new things but she won't listen so the class doesn't listen to her. She keeps saying at least she has two college degrees. What's that supposed to do for us?!

October 30, 1990

Dear Janice,

The music teacher, Mr. Macdougal is on to me. I seem to always start laughing in his class. I'm a soprano and like most other men he's a baritone. His vocal chords weren't made for high notes. He's always demonstrating to the sopranos how high to get up there. It doesn't work well with his voice. Whenever he tries I always laugh. I can't help it. Every week it happens. So now he's always glancing in my direction which only makes me laugh more. I've got to control myself or detention and I will be soon acquainted.

November 2, 1990

Dear Janice,

The eighth grade at J.H.S. 80 are so rude to the teachers! We were at our weekly auditorium period and a teacher got up to speak. They booed and they yelled things out. I felt so bad for the poor man. He's not a very aggressive teacher so he just let it go by, hurting him as it did. Kids today have no respect. Not including me of course. Some of the other kids are like me, and care about other people's feelings but the majority don't seem to have a heart. It's sad, but it's true. We're planning a surprise shower for Rondah. She has no idea we're doing it. It's going to be hard keeping it from her. I usually tell her everything to spare her feelings. On her birthday, thinking she thought no one had gotten her a present, I started telling her what Ninnie (that's what we call our mother) got her. Guess what she said to me?! "Boy, you can't even keep a secret!" There I was trying to make her feel better. I'm using that to inspire me to lie myself to shame when she complains, "My family is so inconsiderate, they won't even throw the bearer of their first grandchild, niece or nephew a shower."

I can't wait to see the look on her face when we yell, "Surprise!" Catch you tomorrow.

November 5, 1990

Dear Janice,

I've got in trouble because of my friends before, but today was different. The reason I'm in trouble is my friend's a boy. He called me and my mother answered the phone. Now she's upset that a boy calls me. She says "she's" not ready for that. Ready for what? I've told her he's my friend but she doesn't seem to want to believe that. I guess she thinks that girls should have girls as friends. I don't agree one bit. I would be ready for a closer relationship with a guy anyways if it was the case. I don't mean really close, but I would be ready to go out with a guy. What I mean by going out is that we would be a couple. We would go places together, he would call me everyday! And yes, we would kiss at times! This subject is so hard to talk about. My mother has put such a spell on me that even talking about boys makes me feel I'm doing something wrong.

When I first got my period, she yelled and yelled at me because she thought I was too young. She made me feel like it was my fault. I'll never forget that day, she said, "You know what comes after this—babies!" She went on and on. I was crying like crazy and she never stopped to even hug me and say things would be okay. That day I thought things wouldn't be right ever again. I wish she never found out. These days sex is everywhere. On t.v. almost everything involves sex. It can't be kept away from me, even though my mom wants it to be. I admit I know everything there is to know about it. None of this knowledge came from my mother. It mostly came from the streets and what I hear everyday.

My opinion is there is no age limit on when to have sex. I think if a person, even one at my age, felt they were ready, and *knew* they were ready, no matter what anyone said, would definitely do it. I'm not sure how I feel, in my situation. I'm all mixed up.

I watch a lot of television and I think I know everything I should know about having a boyfriend. The pains, the joys, etc. I am emotionally ready for that. I know it. Well, anyway, I won't be able to have a boyfriend if my mom won't even let a boy call me! If I meet someone I really like I don't know what will become of us because I would definitely want to talk a lot on the phone.

———— ✇ ✇ ✇ ————

November 7, 1990

Dear Janice,

Winter is the most depressing time of the year. If you go outside at 5:00, darkness is what greets you. It's sickening! I love the summer. Summer to me means no heavy coats, daytime until at least 8 at night and no trembling teeth. I can't wait for June to come around, I was born in June you know. I'll be a teenager next birthday. I like the sound of that. Not that it would mean any more privileges for me, twelve is really no different from thirteen. I would like thirteen to mean I'm a bona fide teenager, not a little kid! I don't want to have to feel bad if I get a crush on a guy for example. It would be so great if I could talk to my mom and say, "I really like this guy at school." She would get upset. I don't want to be an adult or anything I just want to be able to talk to my mom about new found feelings and things like that.

November 9, 1990

Dear Janice,

Today in school the assistant principal was talking about highschool and which ones we should pick to attend. I think it's great we get to pick. It gives us an early start on decision making. There are a lot of choices. I've made my decision a long time ago. It's Bronx Science all the way. It's a top school and it's close. My friend and neighbor Lisa goes there. She likes it. It's her freshman year and she's already feeling at home. I really don't want to go to the closest school which is Evander Childs. By what I've been hearing about it, only a bunch of hooligans go there. I don't want to be a part of it. I hope highschool is different from J.H. I hope it's a more mature atmosphere than J.H.S. 80, I'd do much better. I hope to get a scholarship from highschool to go to a top college.

November 10, 1990

Dear Janice,

Rondah's shower was today. It really turned out good. This morning I thought it would be a disaster. First of all it was raining. That brought down my mood instantly. We decided to keep it at Aunt Mable's house. That's because

38

if we had kept it at our house, she would have found out by our decorating and cooking. We got her friend to say they were going out and we said we were just going to stop by Aunt Mable's. After we were at Aunt Mable's, we called her friend right before they were supposed to leave and asked them if they could drop something off at the house. When they came we yelled, "Surprise!" Rondah looked pretty shocked. She got a lot of presents. There were so many little clothes and things. She said to me, "I'll never trust you again." She was talking about how good I lied. I guess she thinks since I'm such a convincing liar, I've been doing it to her for years.

November 12, 1990

Dear Janice,

One thing I really miss about not staying home in the days is watching my soap operas. And when it comes to soap operas, I think ABC is the best. From "Loving" to "General Hospital" I'm glued to the set. I guess why I like watching them is those are other people's problems on the screen, not yours. You grow to love certain characters, then hate others. But the thing is, you like to hate them. It's hard to explain. I just love television. I'd better start reading some books though. I can't let myself become a t.v.holic. Right now I'm watching Estelle Getty portray Sophia Patrilo on

"The Golden Girls." It's one of those repeats that come on
Fox at 6:00. It's a funny episode.

November 15, 1990

Dear Janice,

I feel like calling Ann (my cousin in Canada). I guess it's
because she's mature and I long for a conversation with a
mature friend. My friends are acting quite the opposite. I
wish she didn't live so far away. She's a real friend to me. It
was in her mother's house that I spent the summer vacation.
We has a lot of fun together. She's 16 and she took me
places and introduced me to all her friends and at night in
the bedroom we'd talk about the old days in Jamaica. We'd
talk about how goofy we were back then compared to now.
I didn't know anything—I couldn't really remember
everybody while she remembered everyone we were ever
acquainted with. She holds that over me. I hope to go back
to Jamaica at Easter. It would be really something to go
back to the old house and see old friends. I only hope they
remember me. I haven't exactly been keeping in touch.
Letters aren't really my thing. I write them but I hardly ever
end up posting them.

⁪ ⁪ ⁪

November 18, 1990

Dear Janice,

I didn't go to church today. I got dressed up and everything but my cousins who I usually go with weren't going so I came back home. I didn't do much back here. I just circulated around this house. The old me would have went straight outside to my friend's house. I find I've lost interest in going outside. I was usually like a magnet drawn to steel when it came to going outside. Now, I could spend a whole week without stepping past the doorstep. Except for going to school of course. I think I've matured somewhat. I always was concerned about what I was missing outside. I never wanted to be left out on anything happening with my friends who are always doing something or going somewhere. In the way I've matured I've come to the sudden realization that there are many more things to life like being close to my family, before it's too late. Pretty soon I'll be off to college, then married with kids. I might be rushing things a bit, but these years go by very fast.

I'm my own person. I like to think that I'm not just my cousin's cousin or my friend's friend. I like to think I'm the individual Latoya Hunter.

November 20, 1990

Dear Janice,

Today Beth, a girl in my class told this boy that I like him. I don't know why she did that. She's always saying I'm too quiet. She's right. I am more than quiet, I'm really shy. There's something about having people looking directly at me, listening to everything I say and waiting for me to say or do something that terrifies me. I usually figit or shake my leg—especially when people are looking at me and focusing their attention on me. For this reason I don't say much except to people I know really well. Anyways, now I've got a boy going around thinking I like him when I don't. It's really getting to his head. He stares at me and when I turn around, he's always there. I don't want to break it to him. One thing about me is I can't give bad news. Then again, maybe it won't be bad news to him. I don't know. Beth won't do it. I really hate her!

There is this one guy I like. His name is Kirk. He's so cute! He's in 8th grade. He's friendly, funny, everything. I think I'll just keep that to myself. I don't want him to know. I just like to secretly admire him, it's probably better that way with all the gossip that goes around schools. Especially when a boy likes a girl.

November 24, 1990

Dear Janice,

My brother is planning an engagement party. It's going to be at his fiancee Michelle's house. She used to live in Brooklyn before she moved in with him so the Bronx posse will have to take their party gear to Brooklyn. I probably won't even go because it starts at 9:00. Michelle says if I go I'll have to go upstairs at 10:00. I hope she wasn't serious. I'd rather stay home than go there and be stuck upstairs. She couldn't have been serious. Anyway, it was the average Saturday. I woke up at 10:00, watched Soul Train in bed, got up, did things around the house until 12:00 and watched Star Search. After that I took a shower, slept, went outside, came back in, slept, and so it goes on. My life can be pretty boring sometimes but what can I say? I'm twelve.

November 26, 1990

Dear Janice,

School is such a bore! Maybe I was just tired today but my eyes kept closing, especially in Social Studies. That teacher could go on and on about things that have nothing to do with S.S. He's just like last year's Spanish teacher. Her name is Miss Waldinger but her students refer to her as Miss

Walding-a-ling. She would go on and on about her life like we really cared if her son got an A on his report card. It was torture to sit in her class. The best part of the 45 minutes she spent with us was when we said "Adios." I guess in every school there's a teacher that qualifies as a sleeping pill.

Home and Careers is an okay class when I think about it. I love to talk about life and learn about life. It's one of the only kinds of learning that gets my mind flowing and eager to know more. Things like how many times the heart beats per minute don't seem important to me. So I'm glad there is a class like Home and Careers that turns on that interest switch in my brain. I can pass tests in the other classes and understand what they teach but it isn't the same.

November 29

Dear Janice,

Today it happened! My sister has brought forth into the world an adorable baby boy named Devoy. I can't believe I've got a nephew. I can't believe my sister has a son. I've never thought of my sister as a mother.

I didn't get a really good look at the little thing. They rolled him by in what looked to me like a glass cage. I don't think my nephew should spend his first hours on the outside world in a glass cage.

When I came home from school my father told me she

went into labor. A thousand different feelings attacked me at once. I was happy I was going to meet my nephew or niece, I was nervous, I was apprehensive, I was sorry for my sister who I knew was in intense pain. For nine months, he was almost like a dream, now he's so real. I know I'll love him to death. I want to have a child as soon as I get out of college and have had a steady job for a year. Hopefully I'll be married and making money so I could give the baby everything she (I hope) wants.

Sunday, November 31, 1990

Dear Janice,

Rondah came home with the baby today. He is so adorable. He's always sleeping and when he is awake, he doesn't open his eyes much but I've still grown to start loving him. I can't wait for him to get bigger so I can take him places and spoil him. I wonder what it will be like having a baby in the house. This is all so exciting. I think everyone feels how I do. My parents seem really happy. My aunts Mable and Rita came over with a few friends. People from around the area also came around to see him. The house has been really busy. When the excitement dies down, I'm prepared for the reality of having a baby around. One thing about me that's helped me out in a new situation is that nothing really takes me by surprise.

December 3, 1990

Dear Janice,

I'm kind of upset right now. It's because of Rondah and her attitude. I can't even touch the baby without her having something to say about it. I understand she's a new mother and she doesn't want anything to happen to her baby, but she's got to loosen up. It's not like I throw him up in the air or make him do somersaults. I just hold him and look at him. My parents tell her to loosen up too but no one can change my sister. I trust my parents as experienced people when it comes to babies, they've had four, but Rondah isn't listening to them about anything.

December 5, 1990

Dear Janice,

Devoy actually stared at me today. He opened his eyes for a while and stared at me. My reaction was to run out of the room. He just looks so creepy. I don't know why. It's just coming to the realization that my sister has really made someone. I never really thought about it. It's such an amazing thing.

In school everything is going on like it always does. The

only difference in my day is I have something more to look forward to going home and seeing my nephew.

December 6, 1990

Dear Janice,

There was a brutal fight after school between two girls. I don't know why but I know one of them didn't want to fight. She was going on the bus when the other girl pulled her off the bus and started beating her like crazy. The other one started fighting back. No one even tried to stop them. It was like boxing, the kids were entertained by watching it. Then blood started to shed. The cops must have smelled the blood because that's when they showed up finally. They put the girl who started it in the car and I don't know where they took her.

December 8, 1990

Dear Janice,

Sorry I didn't talk to you yesterday, I was over at Dave's house. He picked me up last night and brought me home in the morning before he went to work. He's a good brother I think. I'm lucky to have him. Since he moved out I've been over there around three times. Sandra, his girlfriend, and I are really close so I'm not only over there to be with him. If we were alone it would be really awkward. What does a 23 year old guy and his 12 year old sister have to talk about? He'd do much better with a little brother. In fact, when Devoy reaches around 5 years I guess they'll be going around like that. Dave could bring him around and buy him some cool clothes. The other day I heard him say something like that too. I suppose he's very happy to have a little nephew. I wish both my brothers still lived with me. It would be nice having them always around again!

December 9, 1990

Dear Janice,

My cousin and his mother who live in Bermuda have decided to spend Christmas vacation here in N.Y. I can't wait to see him. He was so little when I last saw him. He must be at least seven now.

Anyways, there are 15 days left for Christmas shopping. Rondah is going to put up the tree tomorrow. Every Christmas, the two of us do the honors. We're suppose to have a dinner party at the house on Christmas. That'll be a change. Every Christmas, the Hunters have had to go to one of my mothers two aunts house. This year we'll get to do the entertaining.

December 13, 1990

Dear Janice,

Today Devoy is two weeks old. At the time I'm writing this—8:15 exactly, 14 days ago he was born. I think he actually smiled today. It's probably only gas though. I don't think he has anything to smile about as yet. The only thing he does in life is eat, sleep, and dirty his diapers.

I'm happy my sister doesn't trust me with him enough to

make me change his diapers. I could do it but in her mind, I can't. No arguments here.

Friday, December 14, 1990

Dear Janice,

Today is Friday and my brother Courtney's engagement party is tomorrow. I got a new outfit yesterday to wear there. It's black and white and I think I like it. My sister and I had a hard time choosing. At least I did. I think I'm a hard person to shop for or with. I don't want to be but if I don't like something and buy it anyway, I know it'll spend most of the time in my closet. Anyways, I can't wait for the party. I know it's going to be good.

Sunday, December 16, 1990

Dear Janice,

I was right. The party was wonderful. They had good music and good food. What more can you ask for?

My mother made a toast and in the middle of it started crying. Isn't that sweet? She'll probably do the same thing at the wedding. She's got to look at it this way, she's not losing a son, she's gaining a daughter. I'm gaining a sister. Devoy's gaining an aunt and so it goes on. I think Michelle will be a good addition to the family.

December 17, 1990

Dear Janice,

I have two news flashes. My grandparents are coming from Canada for Christmas, and Sandra (Dave's girlfriend) is having a surprise birthday party for him on the 29th. His birthday is the 25th. I didn't tell you before that he was born on Christmas.

Well, it'll be nice to have my grandparents here to share the holidays. Shane will be here (he's the cousin I said was coming from Jamaica) and we'll all be together. I think my grandmother will be really happy to see Shane. That's her grandchild too and she hasn't seen him for years. By the way, Shane and his mother (my uncle's ex) will be coming the 20th. That's only 3 days from now.

Tuesday, December 19, 1990

Dear Janice,

Tomorrow will be my last day in school before the vacation starts. I go back on the 2nd of January, 1991!! I like the way that sounds.

Anyways I wonder how I'll spend the vacation. Probably in my house but that's OK. Shane will be there. I'm kind of disappointed I won't get to meet them at the airport. They have a 9:30 flight. I'll be in school then but when I get home he'll be there. I hope he remembers me. We lived together for at least 3 years. Surprised? That was in Jamaica. When I left there, he was at least 3 or 4.

December 20, 1990

Dear Janice,

Shane is here! He is so big. I was expecting him to grow a little but not that much as he did. I came home from school and saw him in the living room watching a movie and eating cheese curls. When he saw me he hid his face (I don't know why). I didn't hug him because I didn't know if he remembered me or not. I asked him if he remembered me and he said yes. I could tell he was lying through his teeth. I showed him old pictures of the two of us in Jamaica. I think that helped his memory a little bit. I think I'll like the vacation but one thing though—they've taken over my room. My bed for the next 10 days will be the couch. Lucky me! Whenever there's company, I'm the one who gets dumped in the living room. I hate it so much. It's just another reminder of how powerless I am at this age.

December 21, 1990

Update on Devoy

Devoy is smiling regularly now. I feed him now and sometimes they leave me alone with him. So as you can see, Rondah has really loosened up. I guess it was just a phase.

I found out something new about Shane today. The boy is obsessed with money. He walks around begging for money. I hope it's a habit he'll get over soon. I'm going to take him shopping on Saturday hope he's not as hard to shop with as I am.

Everybody wants money these days. Actually, a better word is "needs." Out of all my friends I'm always the one with money all the time. When we're coming home from school I can always stop and buy junk food if I want. I always give them money to buy something. It's not that I'm rich (definitely not) it's just that my parents give me any spare money they have and it adds up! When things are going really bad financially, it shows on them. I hate to say this but it changes somewhat how nice they act. I hate that money could control things like that, but it does.

My grandparents will be arriving late Saturday night.

Saturday, December 22, 1990

It's 10:00 pm and my grandparents still haven't arrived. Their train was delayed. I'll fill you in on their arrival tomorrow. I did last minute shopping today. I finished for everyone on my list. As I told you, I took Shane. I didn't think it was possible but I've found someone harder to shop with than me. Shane runs through the stores picking every toy he could find. He must have thought I had a million dollars on me. I finally satisfied him with a toy bow and arrow set and an outfit. I don't got a lot of money to shop with so when everyone opens their presents I hope their not overwhelmed with disappointment. The worst of all was what I got Daddy—a pack of white socks. Anyway, for my mother I got a set of purses, for Rondah, a baby album with a family tree on it. As for my brothers I got t-shirts— Courtney's has the Mets on it (he loves the Mets). For their girlfriends I got perfume.

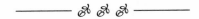

Monday, December 24, 1990

Dear Janice,

My grandparents finally came at 12:00 last night. My grandmother brought cake from Canada that she made herself. She's good in the kitchen. After our reunion we all went over to my Aunt Rita to drop them off. That's where they'll spend the vacation. They'll of course come over every day. Well, tomorrow is Christmas.

Tuesday, December 25, 1990

Dear Janice,

Merry Christmas! It's been one for me. I opened my presents 12:00 last night. I got mostly clothes. That's what I love! They weren't dressy clothes, just clothes I could wear to school. I'm glad because I want to look different in '91. I hate wearing the same set of clothes for too long.

The dinner at the house was a big success. It seemed like the whole family was under our roof. We ate like crazy. We had (I had) curried goat, Ox tail, lasagna . . . It was great. Even though Christmas here in New York can be good, none could top a Jamaican Christmas. It's the best time of the year, back home. On Christmas Eve, parents give their kids money and they go to what we call Christmas Market.

We bought junk food until we were sick and any foolish toys we wanted. I remember how we'd come home and sit outside until it was way too late and just have a good time. Back home, Christmas meant a certain extent of freedom and no limit on the fun. In America it just seems to be restrained to opening some presents and eating alot. You can't go outside and be free and comfortable because it's so cold. A Jamaican night is like a cool bath—it makes you feel renewed and alive. I miss Jamaica on Christmas. I really do.

Wednesday, December 26

Dear Janice,

Today was mostly spent cleaning up the house. It was pretty boring. The excitement of the holidays is slowly disappearing. When my grandparents and Shane and Donna leave, I think that's when it'll be officially gone. For my grandparents that'll be tomorrow and for Donna and Shane, early Sunday morning after the party (the only things left to look forward to). Anyways, I'll talk to you in the morrows (as my brothers would say).

December 28, 1990

Dear Janice,

I went to the movies today with my friends Deborah, Denise, and Isabelle. We saw LOOK WHO'S TALKING II at Dave's girlfriend's theater that she manages in Manhattan. I had a good time but when I got home, I got in trouble for not bringing along Shane. Do you think that was inconsiderate? Maybe it was but I thought Donna (his mother) wouldn't want me taking her son on a NYC subway system alone. I guess sometimes I think too much.

Sunday, December 30, 1990

Dear Janice,

The party was good! It was better than good, I have no word to describe it. I danced all night. I was so relaxed and loose. I really had fun. My brother was surprised I think. Then again maybe he knew all along. You never know. This guy who drank a lot too much kept following me around all night. He kept asking me to dance. He didn't stop until he fell asleep in the kitchen. I'm supposed to know him from Jamaica. His brother and my brother were good friends. He said he always used to come visit up where I lived with his brother. I really don't remember. He does. Anyways, he and his three brothers claim to know me. As I said, I don't remember. I think his other brother Derek likes me. He kept looking at me all night. At first I thought, "This guy is so obvious about being interested in me." He could have kept it in more. It makes me feel like I was under a microscope. There was a little eye contact but he never did say anything to me but the looks he gave me said a thousand words. Oh well, the party was like I said, wonderful.

Donna and Shane left. For me that was a tearful goodbye because I might not see them again for years. At least I've got my room back.

I'll miss them a lot.

Monday, December 31, 1990

Dear Janice,

Today's the last time I'll write 1990 above my entries to you. My resolution this year is not to make any resolutions. I always end up breaking them.

I've got some news for you. Derek, who I told you I thought liked me from the party, called me. Don't even think it. I did not give him my number. I asked him who did and he said it was his brother who is friends with my brother. Anyways, we talked about a lot. We talked about Jamaica mostly and he still insists they know me.

My mother will have a fit if she knows there's a boy

calling me. I know she will soon, but I do not know how pissed off she'll be. I do not want to find out.

P.S. Talk to you in 1991.

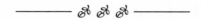

New Years Eve 1990

Dear Janice,

It's a few hours away from 1991. I have nothing to look forward to for the night except babysitting Devoy and watching the countdown on t.v. My mom is going to a party, so is Rondah. Daddy is working. Poor thing, he's worse off than I am. It's really a shame. Actually it's pitiful. But that's my life! Hopefully next year will be much better. I'll be starting out the first hours of it on a boring, depressing note, but that leaves 365 days to make it better. I hate making resolutions because I always break them. Anyway, this year I'll make a resolution not to make any resolutions. Last year I promised myself I would stop eating so much junk food and that I would be neater and more organized. Being that the store is right at the corner from me and I pass it everyday coming from school, the junk food thing didn't last too long. As far as being neat and organized, I just don't think I was made to be neat. I try but it's too much of a strain.

——— ✿ ✿ ✿ ———

January 2, 1991

Dear Janice,

At school it feels so strange to write 1991. I make mistakes and write 1990. That happens every year to me. It takes me a while to get adjusted. I'm trying in school to listen more to the teachers. I think my listening skills are a little weak. It's not really a resolution, it's something I have to do. I realize that I blank out too much. Like I start to listen, and I drift off. What's happening to me? I've thought about it and it's happening so often now. I think about so much. I mostly fantasize. I think back to things that happened before and how I could have acted better in the situation. Like if I had a fight with my mom, I think of what more I could have said to her to get everything off my chest. I often hold things back. Anyway, it's things like that that make me drift. The last thing I need now, is a drop in grades. Now that a guy calls my house regularly, I could just hear my mom, "Now your mind is full up with boys and you can't do your lessons." I don't think that has nothing to do with nothing. Maybe it's a phase.

January 4, 1991

Dear Janice,

Girls in school are so stuck up! They plaster their faces with makeup everyday and finish cans of hairspray every other day. They are so materialistic! Do you know what's in this year? Mirrors. They all carry little mirrors and they stare at themselves almost every minute of the day. It's all for the boys. They put so much into getting guys to like them that is almost scary. Suppose I was like them? What would my mother do? To think of it, she's lucky I'm the way I am, she is more than lucky.

One of the materialistic snob's name is Babette. I hate her! She makes me so sick. She thinks she's better than everybody else. I feel like ringing her neck. She's really beginning to bug me now. In the beginning of the school I wasn't sure how I felt about her, but now I know I can't stand her. The whole problem is her attitude, I think she's some kind of higher force than anything. If it's one thing I hate, it's conceited people. I wish they would transfer her to another class because I don't want to have hostile thoughts when I'm trying to learn.

P.S. I called Derek today.

—————— ✄ ✄ ✄ ——————

January 7, 1991

Dear Janice,

Derek called after school today, he's nice to talk to. I like him. We talk naturally to each other like we've known each other for years and years. Anyways, my mom doesn't know he calls yet. I don't want her to answer the phone one day when he's calling. Who knows what she'll say. I don't want to find out. Rondah is already giving me a hard time about it. I know I'm in for a lot of arguments and maybe I'm just being stupid, but I'm not going to tell him to stop calling. I could be really stubborn sometimes and now is one of those times. I like him, is it a sin? I wish I had a family like my friend Teniesha has. She can even invite boys over to the house and she's younger than me. Her mother is so chill. They wear the same clothes, they go out a lot together, and they talk about anything together. I think Jamaican mothers are more strict about things like boys. Maybe I'm wrong. Maybe it's a universal thing. I don't know. Teniesha is so lucky! She's always so happy, she never seems to have any problems with her family. I really envy her.

January 9, 1991

Dear Janice,

Today gunshots echo in my head. They are the same gunshots that killed an innocent human being right across from my house last night. They are the same gunshots that have scarred me, I think, forever.

Late last night, I was in bed when I heard a man screaming for a police officer. I told myself, I didn't hear that. Later I told myself I didn't hear the four gunshots that followed his cry for help. I lay there in bed and it was like I was frozen. I didn't want to move an inch. I then heard hysterical crying. I ran to the window when I couldn't keep myself back any longer. What I saw outside were cops arriving. I ran into my parent's room and woke them up. By that time, tears were pouring unstoppably from my eyes. I couldn't stop shaking. My parents looked through the window and got dressed. They rushed outside and I followed them. It turned out that I knew the person who got shot. He worked at the store at the corner. He was always so nice to me, he was always smiling. He didn't know much English but we still managed a friendship.

I can't believe this happened. Things like this happen everyday in N.Y., but not in my neighborhood, not to people I know.

January 11, 1991

Dear Janice,

Today the store was closed. It was closed yesterday also. The blood stains are still across the street. In school I couldn't stop thinking about what happened, yesterday was the same thing. I don't think I'll get over this for a long while.

The whole neighborhood is talking about it, some say one thing and others say something else. They say the murderers were waiting for him in his van. He and his partner were going into the van when the murderers came out. That's all that has been said about it. I don't think drugs had anything to do with it—the guy was just too sweet. When I listen to them yapping away about it, I don't mention that I heard a thing when it happened. They're only interested in the facts of the matter. I'm interested in the heart of it. It really makes me think why did it happen to such a sweet, innocent guy? He didn't deserve it.

--- ᚙ ᚙ ᚙ ---

January 12, 1991

Dear Janice,

The store was opened today. There were a lot of people standing around in there. Not necessarily buying anything, they just stood around. Fernando, a young friendly guy who works in the store who was always very cheerful, was not as cheerful today. His eyes were red and swollen and he just kind of moped around. The funeral is Saturday and they're asking for donations. I wouldn't feel right going to his funeral. I think funerals should be for the really close family of the dead. Those whose goodbye would mean the most to him. I have nothing to donate so my parents donated some money. All I have is deep sympathy and sadness for the loss of a friendly person who always put a smile on my face.

--- ᚙ ᚙ ᚙ ---

January 14, 1991

Dear Janice,

I've been so caught up in the murder shock that I've forgotten to update you on school. A really good saxophone player came to school to perform. His name is Naji. The school loved him. He is really talented. I have a feeling he's going to make it big in the music industry.

You don't know this but when I was ten I used to play the drums at P.S. 94. It was really easy; as my music teacher said, you've just got to have rhythm. This year however, I'm stuck in vocals as you know.

January 15, 1991

Dear Janice,

Since the murder I haven't been particularly interested in going outside. Today I was thinking about everything. My friends have been doing things and I haven't been there. They'll tell me what's happened the previous day, and I'll feel left out. I was thinking I shouldn't spend so much time in the house anymore. I think tomorrow I'll go outside for a while. This is going to sound funny but for every car that passes me by while I'm walking down the street, a thought comes to me. It says "I'm going to die now, the person in the car is going to pull out a gun and shoot." The funny thing is when that thought occurs, I don't feel scared that much. I feel calm and ready to face my death. I've discovered about myself that when the day of my death comes, I'll be ready and I'll have a calm soul.

January 16, 1991

Dear Janice,

I hung out with my friends today and must admit had a good time. I think I'm not as conscious of simple things like cars driving by as I was just 24 hours ago. I'm still conscious of people who look suspicious but that's natural for everyone I think. There's a guardian angel in the store at the corner now. Guardian angels are guys who volunteer to protect people who need protection. There are a lot of them in my neighborhood. Other neighborhoods have them too. They go out with taxi drivers in NYC. They started when there was the string of killings of taxi drivers. My personal opinion is the robber will just shoot the taxi driver and the guardian angel and go on with their life.

January 17, 1991

Dear Janice,

Today was a particularly good day. School was fun especially Gym. We played soccer and my team won 8 to 2. We are good!

At the homefront, Courtney and Michelle came over. It's always fun when they come over. Courtney is funny as always and I find fun in bugging Michelle. Dave has not been visiting too often lately. I understand he's busy but he should try to make more time for his family. Especially his little sister who's missing him very much.

January 21, 1991

Dear Janice,

Today someone who's in Mr. Pelka's sixth grade class this year told me some terrible news. Mr. Pelka has pneumonia. He hasn't been working for the past week. I hope it's not a severe case. I'd hate it if anything would happened to him.

January 23, 1991

Dear Janice,

Pneumonia is definitely in season. I just heard that my little cousin Larry is in the hospital suffering from it. He's only 8 months old, I hope he can fight it. He's been sick before. When he was around one month old, he was in the hospital. I remember his mother (my cousin) was telling my sister and me how many hours she spent in the hospital waiting room worrying. I pray to God I never go through anything like that in my life. I pray my life doesn't have any obstacles in it. I really don't think I'm the kind of person that can cross obstacles.

February 1, 1991

Dear Janice,

It's the first day of February. I hate this month. It just seems so long. I think it'll be really boring. It's getting closer to the wedding though. I'm really happy about that. There's a girl in my school who actually had a baby already. She's in the ninth grade, she's probably around 15. My friends were talking about her today. I feel really sorry for her, it's too early! She is only in Junior High! I wonder how it happened. I mean, I know how it happened, but how could she let it? Her mom must have been so upset. I would never do that to my mother. This really makes me thing about this whole sex business. I wonder if that girl was ready. I know I talked about a person feeling that they're ready and doing it. Maybe she thought she was and really wasn't and maybe she knew she she was and still knows she is but just isn't ready for a child. I think being ready for sex and ready for a child are two different things. To be ready for sex, you must have the ability to fall in love and feel close to the maximum to the person you are with. To be ready for a baby, you should be able to take care of yourself and the child and know what's right and what's wrong. You should be able to devote yourself to the child in every way possible. The thing I would say should have been taken care of by that girl is protection. Ready or not ready, she should have thought about that.

February 2, 1991

We went looking for a bridesmaid dress for the wedding today. We have to order them early so they'll come in on time. Well, we settled for a bluish, greenish one. It is so pretty! We wear this big blown out slip underneath it. It's really big and takes up a lot of room but we like it. We drove all the way to Brooklyn. That is like an hour and a half of driving. I hate taking long rides. There was so much traffic it was unbelievable! I would hate to live in Brooklyn. It's dirty, it's ugly, and it's crowded. That's my opinion and I think anybody would say so if they saw Flatbush Avenue. It's so unattractive!

February 3, 1991

Dear Janice,

I went to church today and I really believe I was touched by the Holy Ghost. I think there is really such a thing. I felt it there. Sometimes I get so confused about these things. My grandparents are bona fide Christians so I was grown to believe in God, but I never really thought about the whole concept. There was a really cute, young guy and the spirit struck him. He fell on the floor and he was shaking, and bobbing his head. No one could get him up. Nobody can tell me that was not real. All I could do is look. Sometimes that's all you could do.

I wonder what God thinks about what the world has come to. He must feel really let down. The powers of evil seem to be taking over. It's so scary.

February 5, 1991

Dear Janice,

I started praying last night. It felt so great. It's like he's really there listening to me. I'm going to start doing it regularly. God is up there, I know it. School is going good now. I'm on the honor roll. God must have had something to do with it. All my success, I should dedicate to him. I wonder what happens after you die; they say he takes your soul. That part is really confusing, but I'll just wait until I die to get into that part. Right now I'll just have to live and be the best I could be for him.

February 7, 1991

Dear Janice,

It's amazing how Derek and me have gotten used to each other. We argue a lot now. I'm always hanging up the phone on him. It's fun. We both know one of us will end up calling one another back. It's crazy. Today I hung up on him and I guess he thought it was funny. He kept calling back and hanging up when I picked up the phone. My father was right next to the phone. He was trying to sleep. Derek didn't know that. I got really upset with him though. He's so childish sometimes. He acts really immature. Why do I put up with him? We're actually closer than any of any of my friends and me are. I tell him everything. Maybe too much.

I wonder when exactly did he become part of my life.

February 9, 1991

Dear Janice,

Rondah had decided to start back at college for a degree in business. Starting Monday she won't be home from 4–10. You know what that means—babysitting til I drop.

I'm glad Rondah didn't decide to end her life right here because she had Devoy. I'm glad she wants to become better and expand herself. She is really lucky to have parents like ours and a sister like me who'll babysit for her anytime without pay. I'm becoming quite the little babysitter these days. I can't believe once she didn't want me to even hold the baby. It's nice to know she trusts me with Devoy because I love him to pieces and she knows it.

February 11, 1991

Dear Janice,

We're getting ready for a show in school. The show is all the way in June but the chorus has to learn the songs. I hate how we sound. We are pathetic! I don't like anything about this school. Do you notice that? Everything is so against my taste. The way they teach is one. I mentioned before about English. They don't make me interested in learning. Another thing is the level of maturity among the students. Sometimes I feel going to a prep school would be better for me. I think there is much more seriousness about life in those schools. At my school they would call kids at those schools nerds. If that's the case, nerds are much better off than they are.

I wish I could switch schools. There must be better schools around with better programs and things like that. I didn't have a choice for this school—it's closest to me so this is where I have to go. When I get older, I'm going to make sure I give my kids a choice in what they do. Like what school they think is best for themselves and so on. I want to be able to be such a great parent. I want to have really happy kids. All the things I never had, I'll make sure they have it. I hope my daughter won't have to complain so much in her diary.

February 13, 1991

Dear Janice,

It's coming around the time for Damon's birthday. Who's Damon? Well he's this babyfaced guy who really liked me once. That's when I was around nine. He was my first encounter with boys. In those times when I thought of boys I said, "Eeew." Well, this guy didn't think of girls that way. He was like eleven then. Now listen to what an eleven-year-old boy got me. He got me a gold chain and a two finger ring that said "I Love You." It's hard to believe but it's true.

He was so cute and so sweet and all that I was scared. I ended up giving back his ring and burying the chain. I couldn't be seen with them. My mother would hunt him and his mother down and throw the gifts in their faces. I buried the chain and said me and my next door friend Lisa had become soul sisters by burying the things we held most dear.

Anyway, he really wanted to kiss me and no matter what, I wouldn't let him. Once I went for his cheek to give him a friendly kiss and he went for the lips. I remember wiping and wiping them off after he left. I was so silly.

He's not around anymore. His mom died and he lives in a foster home now. It's a tragic story but it's good to have these memories.

February 16, 1991

Dear Janice,

Rondah's deciding to go back to school had me thinking that I shouldn't waste the opportunity I have now to go to school. I don't remember mentioning that I'm in a special program at school that skips me from 7th to 9th grade. I never mentioned that at school I'm thought of as smart. Teachers think so, students think, nerd. I don't think I'm really a nerd, I just understand the work more than most kids do and I remember things well. Anyway, that's why I'm skipping a grade. The great thing about it is I get out of this dumpy school one year earlier. I can't say I'm definitely going to Bronx Science but it is a dream of mine. The only thing that I think would stop me is if I don't pass the admissions test. That's my one worry. I'll just have to study hard.

February 18, 1991

Dear Janice,

Since Dave's party Rondah has been seeing a lot of this guy named Phillip Osavio. They met there and since then he's been over at the house a lot. He seems really sweet. He dresses nice, wears expensive clothes and has a lot of jewelry. I know the first thing people say when they see a young black guy with things like that is that he's a drug dealer. Phillip is definitely no such thing. He works up in White Plains in this big supermarket. I'm not sure what he does, but Derek used to work for him. That's how Phillip ended up at that party—through his contacts with Derek's bigger brother. Anyway, Phillip told me how Derek used to sit in the back and eat ice cream all day. I think it was a cross between Derek being fired and quitting, but however it happened, he doesn't work there anymore.

—— ⚵ ⚵ ⚵ ——

February 20, 1991

Dear Janice,

I realize I haven't written to you about my big diet I went on. It lasted for a week and that was it. I have no will power whatsoever. I'm thinking back to this diet because when I weighed myself today I was 120! I'm almost ashamed to say it. During those long days of school a person could get a little hungry you know, and I pass at least three stores on my way home from school. That's my excuse for my weight gain, Janice. I've noticed that diets don't work for me, so I'll leave it up to fate.

The other day I went into the store where that man was killed. I hate to say "that man"—he was so friendly—but I never learned his name. Anyway, the loss of his presence is still strong. Things have been getting back as normal as it can be. I still contribute a lot to their cash register.

February 22, 1991

Dear Janice,

My cousin Dexton's (who lives in Canada) birthday was four days ago. I feel bad sometimes when things come up and we don't remember. Whenever we have a birthday on this side of town, there's always a call or a card. My family don't seem to be into things like that. Sometimes I think we're not family-oriented enough. I guess it's because we live in such a fast-paced city but we should sometimes slow down for family. That's a message for everybody—slow down for family.

February 25, 1991

Dear Janice,

Rondah and I seem to have drifted apart after Devoy was born. She's so into the baby now there's hardly room for me. I'd really hate to see our relationship fall apart. Before I left for school she rised to sometimes comb my hair. Today she just sent me out of the room when I asked her. She should rest while she can I understand, but I can't help missing the way things used to be. I can't help it.

February 28, 1991

Dear Janice,

February is coming to an end. March is almost here, then comes April. To me the word April now means wedding.

The months are really flying by. 1990 was a fast-paced year. The fastest since I was born. It seems '91 will be even faster. At least my life doesn't seem to be dragging on and on. My life might have its many many faults, but it really isn't as bad as some people's.

March 2, 1991

Dear Janice,

This Saturday was like all my Saturdays. It seemed really long. I long for a good party. I want to go out and enjoy myself. Listen to me—I'm twelve and talking like I should be partying every night. Sometimes I forget how young I am. It's like at times a 21-year-old mind replaces my regular one. It happens really often. Sometimes I wonder if I'm the only person like this. I hate being young! I hate it with a passion. I'd give anything to be older. I want to be free and make my own decisions. If only that could be!

March 4, 1991

Dear Janice,

I'm feeling good today. After yesterday at church I feel at peace with myself. It's like I'm renewed. I've been telling people how I've found the Lord. They say I shouldn't play with God meaning I shouldn't go around talking about how touched I am when I know I'm not. Well, even if this turns out to be a phase, I know right now I'm really close to God. I was singing negro-spirituals and hymns all day. I feel it from my soul when I sing them. God is really powerful. He's like inside people.

March 6, 1991

Dear Janice,

The world is so sin-corrupted. I guess this is coming from my new religious awareness but it's really true. These days no one thinks about God or following his rule. People kill, back and forth, even those who think they have a right. Like mothers who kill their unborn child. They give it a fancy name—abortion, but I think murder is a much better word for it. The child may be unborn but it is still a person who has the right to a life. If the mother doesn't want to be a part of it why doesn't she give it up for adoption or give it to a home that will care for it? I think it's a very sinful act and it sickens me to hear about it. The number one argument these people keep saying is it's their body. Well, to me, the baby inside them is the one who should say that. Who gives the mother the right to terminate its life?

March 9, 1991

Dear Janice,

The wedding is really coming up quickly. I had no idea so much money was needed for one wedding. The cake alone costs a fortune. There's so much to be done, but I know with both families working at it, it'll get pulled off.

I've been picturing how it's going to be. More like fantasizing, actually. My friends all want invitations. I want them to go but it's not up to me. Courtney and Michelle don't want it too overcrowded. To me, the more the better. I hope it won't be like the weddings on t.v. I don't want a stuck up kind of thing. I want everyone to get down and have fun. I want Jamaican music blasting at the reception and a lot of dancing and noise.

───── ✿ ✿ ✿ ─────

March 11, 1991

Dear Janice,

I'm such a klutz! In gym class I can hardly do anything. I hate playing any sports except basketball. I admit I've become a lot more open to sports since I started this school but that doesn't mean I can play them.

Today I was playing baseball not because I wanted to but because the teacher made me. I got a good chance to out the other team by catching the ball, but when it came to me, I dropped it. This girl started saying, "You're so stupid," and all this other crap. I swear at that moment there was almost smoke coming out of my ears. She's a real little . . . (I won't say). I really feel like ringing her neck until she's drenched of all life.

Anyways, on a happier note, Mr. Pelka is doing much better—remember, I told you he had pneumonia? My cousin Larry is also recovered. There's one thing I don't have to worry about anymore!

March 13, 1991

Dear Janice,

Kirk, whom I have an extreme crush on had his arm around me today. I couldn't believe what was happening. It took me by surprise. I was walking and he just came up beside me and put his arm around me. I didn't know what to say or do. He said, "Hug me back." I was dumbstruck so I just did it kind of unconsciously. He said, "Tighter" (my heart was running a marathon by now). Anyway, I did. After that he just went off somewhere. I still can't believe it. One thing I know is I want this to be the beginning of a beautiful friendship. He's really nice, and so cute! Derek is really close to me though. We talk for hours on the phone and everything but he never made my heart run a marathon. There's a difference there but I don't know which I prefer.

March 15, 1991

Dear Janice,

Kirk pretty much ignored me today. I guess it was a one moment fling. Oh well, that's life. Actually I hate life, if this is what it's supposed to be—disappointments all the time and let downs. Kirk isn't really that important, I just have a crush on him. I'm not going to cry over any guy at anytime—maybe my husband, when I get married. For now, boys are the last thing I want to cry about.

Anyway, maybe Kirk was just too preoccupied today to look my way. You never know.

March 18, 1991

Dear Janice,

Kirk said hi today that's about it. I love the way he walks. I don't know how to describe it. I could just sit back and watch him walk and I wouldn't get bored. I guess that's really silly, but hey, what can I say?

We're learning about the reproductive system in school. The guys in my class act so silly about it. They are so immature. Sometimes I wonder about what goes on in their minds. They are just so predictable. Kirk is older so I guess that's one of the things I like about him. I don't usually get crushes on guys my age. I could see myself at 21 marrying a man who's 35.

March 20, 1991

Dear Janice,

There is this really playful and pretty girl or should I say woman I know named Laura. I would love to get her into my family. There's something about her that I really like. I've been seeing a lot of her lately—she visits sometimes—she's helping me prepare this diary for when it gets published. Anyways, I know in a while we won't be seeing each other, so I was thinking. I thought about her joining my family through my brother Dave. They're the same age and everything! I think it would be so great if they got together. There's one thing though that I should mention—she's white. But to me, it doesn't matter. She's just cool and she could be any color and still be cool. In other words, she'd be a cool black chick as well as she is a cool white one.

Anyway, I don't mean I want her to turn black, but I'm saying I would accept her as part of the family like nothing was different. I won't even mention this to Laura and Dave, but if it was meant to be, fate will do its job.

March 22, 1991

Dear Janice,

I'm doing pretty okay in school I must say. Report cards came out. I didn't get anything below an 80. My mother isn't too proud about it. She says there are not enough 95's and 100's. Unbelievable! She wants and wants and wants.

———— 🚲 🚲 🚲 ————

March 23, 1991

Dear Janice,

We fitted our dresses for the wedding today to see how they'll look. I think it's gorgeous and when I look really close, the dress looks good on me, but when I see my face, it looks dull. Maybe it's the color of the dress but I know I'll definitely have to wear a lot of makeup that day. I wonder when my mom is going to make me wear makeup regularly. I hope soon. Girls at school wear it but they overdo it! They look like paintings. It's not the way I want to look.

March 25, 1991

Dear Janice,

I love Devoy so much. He's growing up so fast. I guess I don't talk about him much. He's become such a big part of my life. I can't wait to see him walking and talking. I hope he calls me Aunty. I also hope he will think of me as someone he has to listen to, not a kid like I've been thought of as being for all my life. When I was talking the other day about abortion, I was thinking of him. What if Rondah had done that? There would be no Devoy now.

March 27, 1991

Dear Janice,

Today at lunch Kirk came and sat beside me. Well I guess he's done ignoring me because he put his leg over my leg. Now this was too much. I would have let him keep it there if I was like Jeanine. She's a really whorey girl. She goes around sitting on guys and touching them up. Anyway, I pushed it off. Then Jeanine came by. She put her arm around it. Later that lunch period, Kirk's cousin told me that Kirk and Jeanine made out in his building. There goes everything.

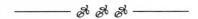

March 29, 1991

Dear Janice,

Rondah's new boyfriend is such a good chef. He cooked us a feast today. It was so good. He seems to be good at a lot. I feel we have a lot in common. He dresses hip, he listens to the music I like and everything. He's perfect. She better hold on to him.

March 31, 1991

Dear Janice,

April is practically here. Once again thoughts of the wedding dance in my head. I'm so much looking forward to this. Rondah's planning to sing. She has a pretty nice singing voice. She's rewriting a gospel song to fit the occasion. I hope she does well up there.

I hope I do well too. I hope I don't act stupid when I have to walk up the aisle! Please God, don't make me mess up!

April 1, 1991

Dear Janice,

It's April Fools! I don't really like to fool around on this day though. My great grandmother was born today. She died when I was around six, but when she was alive, she was really special.

What I remember most about her is she really seemed to love me. The day of her funeral I had a dream about her and since that bees have always been attracted to me. I know it sounds weird but in the dream she came to me and said from now on she would come to me as a bee and she'd always look out for me. I'm serious about this! Ever since that bees are always following me and sometimes I say to them "Hi Granny." Strange it is, but I really believe this.

Happy Birthday Granny!

April 3, 1991

Dear Janice,

School is such a drag! Whenever I look forward to things, anything that comes before it seems to drag and drag.

I'm looking forward to the wedding—it better turn out good! I have such high hopes for it. A part of me wants the excitement to go on and on, the other part wants it to be all over. That's just a small part though. This wedding is all I can think of and talk about. It's getting to my head!

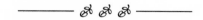

April 5, 1991

Dear Janice,

It's Courtney's wedding day eve. I think I'm as nervous as he is. I take that back. He's a wreck! I'm quarter way to a wreck.

The rehearsal went well. I hope tomorrow will go on the same pace. I'm at Michelle's house right now as are all the other bridesmaids. Michelle is sleeping and the rest of us are watching t.v. It's 12:30 in the morning!

I don't think Michelle is really sleeping. She's probably just lying and thinking.

   ℔ ℔ ℔

April 6, 1991
(early morning)

Dear Janice,

In only a few hours my brother will say his I dos. I can't
help but be nervous. I'm in Brooklyn at the moment.
The rehearsals went on really well. I'm walking with
Michelle's cousin Chris. He's 23 but he's my height. The
way we walk is he puts his hand over mine and we go down
the aisle. When we reach the end we turn to each other. He
bows and I curtsy. It's really cute.

   Well, it's like 12:30 a.m. and this house is packed!
Michelle's relatives from all over the place are here. I don't
know where I'll sleep. I guess right here on the couch. All
the bridesmaids are here except one who lives close by. The
plan for tomorrow is at 5:00 a.m. we will get up and go get
our hair fixed at the hairdresser, after that we'll go fix things
up at the reception hall. After that we'll come back to the
house and get dressed. The limos will come pick us up and
we'll be off to the church. I wonder what Courtney is feeling
right now. He must be so nervous! He's that type that gets
really jumpy. Michelle is calm now but I guarantee she'll be
a mess of nerves tomorrow.

   My cousins, aunt, and grandparents came in from Canada
earlier today. I wish I was up in the Bronx with Ann. I want
to spend as much time as I can with her. She was at the
rehearsals watching and giving me tips. I think I'll make her
my maid of honor at my wedding which I calculate will be

8 years from now. I want to get married at 20 or even 21.
I want to have a huge wedding with 500 guests. So I suppose
I would have to become a millionaire between now and age
20. It's not impossible, if everything fails there's always the
good old lottery. Well, I'll write to you tomorrow after the
big event. Tonight I'm going to pray it'll turn out good. I'm
so nervous.

April 6, 1991 (Saturday night)

Dear Janice,

I t's all over. The wedding bells have rung. The service was
a lot of things but most of all, long! So many things
seemed to come before the minister said "I now pronounce
you man and wife." My feet were killing me, I felt like going
out and sitting in the audience. Being a bridesmaid isn't all
the glamour it seems to be. I gave out so many fake smiles to
so many cameras today, I think I'll never smile again. Those
were the not so good parts but everything else was just great.
Michelle looked gorgeous. Courtney looked handsome.
They took their vows and now they are man and wife.
Another Hunter is added to the family tree. I'm really happy
for them.

I was so nervous at first walking down the aisle but about
halfway down I heard my grandmother calling to me and
cheering me on and I felt better. Everyone was there and

they all looked good. It's so nice that they turned up. Some travelled from as far as Canada and England. (By the way, today was the first time I rode in a limo and hopefully not the last. It was really nice.) About the reception . . . it was fun. My mom made her toast and she did really well. Dave did too. I think what he said was, "I'd just like to say I'm really happy for my brother," then finished with, "That's it." He was never a master when it came to words but, come on! However, I know he meant it. I think he's really proud. We're also glad Michelle's now in our family.

Rondah catched the bouquet! That means she's up next. I certainly hope so. Janice, there a lot more details to tell, but not right now. Tomorrow is another day. My aunt has decided to leave on Monday instead of tomorrow. So, Ann and I will spend time together after all. It was a lovely day and sadly it has to end now.

April 7, 1991

Dear Janice,

Ann and I were together all day. The whole day was really busy. I wasn't really working, but when you have guests, days seem busy. You always have to make sure they are happy. My mom was really getting on top of my nerves this evening. I think when a lot people are around it gets to her head. I didn't like her at all today. It happens sometimes that you love a person but sometimes you just don't like them. It's all very complex.

Ann and I went out for a while, when we came back she was making her noise and that's the last thing I wanted to hear. I wanted to enjoy my time with her. I went on the phone and I made her talk to Derek, she thinks he's a nice person too. Well anyway, my mom was yelling at me to get off the phone. You have no idea how irritating she gets sometimes.

Right now the men in the family are in the living room watching wrestling and my mom, aunt, and grandmother are talking in my parent's room. I love it when everyone is in the same house. Did I ever tell you that? It's one of my favorite feelings. It's like when people take drugs and they get high, but my high is a safe, loving high. I wonder if I'm the only person in the world who feels that way. The love birds, Courtney and Michelle were here today. Their first day married and where are they? At their parent's house. What a bummer! They're putting off their honeymoon for a while because the wedding was such a big expense that they need to wait. They have a special glow to them I never saw before. Everything is going great around this side of town. I wish my relatives didn't have to go back to Canada tomorrow. I'm going to have to go to school but they'll be here when I get back. They're leaving around five. Like somebody once said, all good things must come to an end.

April 8, 1991

Dear Janice,

The house is so dead now. It's moments like this that I feel like crying. They all left me—why did they have to leave? It's not fair. My life is back to its normal, boring self again. I shouldn't really say that. Jamaica is coming up soon. Not soon enough though. I'll know by tomorrow when I'll be leaving. Rondah's going to a travel agent today.

Did I ever tell you how sometimes I miss Jamaica not in the normal but in a gut wrenching way. My brother rented a video one night and it showed an outdoor festival in Jamaica that had a lot of performers in it. It was in the night time in Jamaica and just the way it looked made me want to cry. I wanted to be right out there. I'm not sure what it was; it was how the night looked, I think. Is that strange or what? The night just brought on a certain feeling. The way the trees looked far away behind the stage, just brought me back to how, when I was back home, I used to love to go out, anywhere at all, as long as it was in the night. That day watching the video, I felt so homesick. I think it was the worst case of homesickness ever in history. I just can not wait to go back. I don't just want to go, I *need* to go.

─────── ❧ ❧ ❧ ───────

April 10, 1991

Dear Janice,

We'll be leaving the 23rd. That's 13 days from now. We got the flight booked and everything is set. School will just have to go on without me for two weeks. I'm really excited. I need clothes! I need a lot of summer clothes because as everyone knows, the sun's always shining in Jamaica. I remember when I saw snow for the first time. In Jamaica, the closest anyone came to snow was if they got married and people threw rice at them. When it snowed for the first time when I came here, it was so pretty. The houses were covered and the ground was like a big white blanket. It was gorgeous. I loved it. Now when I walk home from school in the snow and it's like ice, and it stings my face as it blows, I say it'll be better if I was in Jamaica dreaming about it.

I'll have to tell my teachers about me leaving. I guess they would want to give me work to do to keep up while I'm gone. I'm going to miss a major Social Studies test and Reading but I'll make them up when I get back. My mom isn't on it all the way for me to go because she thinks I'll miss too much work but I begged her so she said okay. She could be cool sometimes.

April 13, 1991

Dear Janice,

J ust last week I was a princess for a day in that beautiful
dress and parading in a limo. This week I'm just a plain,
boring twelve-year-old. Yuck!

I wouldn't mind doing it again. Michelle says so too. She
said her dress is way too expensive to put away forever. I
agree. I want to feel like a princess for forever and a day.

April 15, 1991

Dear Janice,

E ight days left until Jamaica. My mother got me some
summer clothes to wear while I'm down there. I'll be in
90 degree weather in less than a week and now I'm in 30
degree weather. It'll only take like four hours to reach from
here to there. Thank goodness for technology. We've come
a long way since the day of horseback.

I can't wait for these eight days to be over. Here I go
again, it's like the wedding—until it comes I think of
nothing else.

—— ❦ ❦ ❦ ——

April 17, 1991

Dear Janice,

E ven though I'll miss a lot of school, at this point I don't
care! All I want is to be there in Jamaica. Kids I told at
school that I'm leaving envy me. While they're busting their
brains I'll probably be on the beach. Lucky me! Poor them!
I'm really happy for myself.

—— ❦ ❦ ❦ ——

April 19, 1991

Dear Janice,

J amaica doesn't seem too far away now. Rondah and I
confirmed our tickets today. In the beginning Rondah
wanted everyone to go, but it ended up working down to just
me, her, and Devoy. It will be so nice to get away from this
place for a few weeks. I don't think I'll miss anyone to be
very honest. Maybe I'll miss the presence of them but not
the idea of them. I definitely won't miss my parents telling
me what to do and what not to do every minute. That's
exactly what I want to get away from. It seems like
everything I really want, not always material things, but
things I want to do or experience, I never get. I know they
have their parental reasons, but I have my adolescent
reasons.

Like today I was talking on the phone and my mother just grabbed it and was about to say something to really embarrass me. Before she had the chance I just hung up the phone. It was Derek and I guess she knew. Embarrassing isn't quite the word I should have used. By the way she grabbed the phone she was going to say something like "get off the phone" and then hang up.

I know she doesn't approve of him or anything but come on! She wants me to respect her but she doesn't respect me. When I'm doing innocent things like talking on the phone, and she makes me feel like I'm doing the worst thing in the world, it makes me want to go out and really do something! She sits on top of my every nerve. Today I just felt like leaving, that feeling is becoming a regular thing for me.

April 20, 1991

Dear Janice,

Derek got jumped today. They took his jacket and his money. When I first called, he was like, "I can't talk right now." I was mad because I thought he was just trying to get out of talking to me. I said something like, "Don't call me back," and hung up. When he did call, I found out the reason he couldn't talk was because he was bleeding. He said he was walking home by himself and about six guys attacked him. I felt so bad. He tried to play tough guy, but I know he was shaken up. All I could say was I'm sorry. He didn't want to talk about it, I suppose he wanted to forget it. I'm glad he didn't want to discuss it because I didn't know what to say. It's like a girlfriendly duty to comfort a guy. I don't have any experience in things like that—I'm just really angry at whoever did it! Poor thing! It always happens to the good guys!

On another note, I told my teachers at school that I was leaving and they didn't hesitate to swamp me with homework. Oh, well. It's still the school year, what did I expect?

April 21, 1991

Dear Janice,

I don't know what's going on with me. I really try to be a good daughter, I try to get good grades at school, I come home every day in one piece, and I would never do anything to hurt or harm anyone. Is there anything more I need to do? It's just that whatever I do, I always feel like I haven't done enough to please everyone around me. It's not that I want desperately to please everybody, it's just that I feel I have to get approval.

With my mother it's like I can't please her. She was looking in my notebook and she saw two tests. On one of them I had 100 percent and on the other one I had a 95.

When she turned to that one she turned to her friend and said "she's getting so backwards, it's like she's not learning anything." It was only five points. With her it seems they all have to be hundreds. She says I'm going to end up cleaning floors for a living. What kind of words are those to live by?

I love my mother but sometimes she makes me feel less than I really am.

Anyways, tomorrow I'll be one day away from being away from it all.

———— ✃ ✃ ✃ ————

April 22, 1991

Dear Janice,

Tomorrow is the big day. Even though this packing I'm doing is driving me crazy, it doesn't feel so bad because tomorrow I'll be in Jamaica! I'm still trying to get used to the thought. I just know it's going to be good. As soon as that plane lands tomorrow, I'll know I'm home, or at my second home I should say. I'll talk to you tomorrow.

—— ❦ ❦ ❦ ——

April 23, 1991

Dear Janice,

I do not know how to start this entry. Should I start out by telling you about the horrible and life threatening plane ride, or about the beautiful place I'm writing from? I think I'll start with the ride.

Janice, for a moment or should I say quite a few moments in the plane ride I thought it would be the end of Rondah, Devoy, myself and everyone else on flight. Somewhere between America and Jamaica the plane started shaking violently. Some of the containers from the breakfast that had just been served just started falling over. The pilot was repeating over and over again the everyone had to remain in their seats with their seatbelt fastened. He said we were in a very dangerous situation.

Maybe what happened was just another common case of turbulence but you really think about your life when you feel it's going to end in a few moments. The first people I thought about I think are the most important to me at this stage in my life. Up there thinking I was going to die I thought of Rondah, sitting beside me praying as it looked like, Devoy sleeping in her lap (that kid sleeps through anything), and my parents who were unaware of everything going on. I thought of my brothers of course, who I pray will only be taken from my life when my life is taken.

Those people I always knew were important. I thought of my other relatives of course. My new sister Michelle was in my thoughts too, that was no surprise. A surprise though was that Derek was one of the first. My mother would kill me on the spot if she knew this but I just got to tell someone my feelings about Derek. Over the four months I've known him or have gotten to know him and understand him, I've really grown attached to him. Just to hear his voice on the phone makes my days complete. I don't know what you call these feelings I have. It's just so new to me. Whenever I talk to him I feel important. He makes me feel like I count in his life. I suppose that is the reason he's special—he makes me feel special. If there's any guy I should be kissing, it's him. He'll always be sort of like a first love. Why am I talking about Derek when I'm on a gorgeous island? I don't know. It's one of those things that I can't understand.

April 24, 1991

Dear Janice,

Today I spent settling into my home for the next fourteen days. Rondah went out with friends and I had to baby-sit. My aunt was kind enough to allow my cousin Oudia to stay home with me. I was so bored! I was hot, drowsy, and cranky. I couldn't really go out or even take a walk because Devoy would be too much trouble. It was an all in all terrible day. Tomorrow however, will be better. Rondah and I are going to stay up in St. Ann until Saturday.

As you know that's where I was born and raised. I can't believe I'll actually be going back there. I can't wait to get there and visit my old teachers and all my friends. And of course Janice, Janice. I'm going to see the person I named you after.

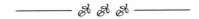

April 25, 1991

Dear Janice,

Today was mostly filled with disappointment. I don't know where to begin. I'm not writing to you from my old home in St. Ann, but instead my Aunt's house in St. Catherine. The three day trip to St. Ann where I would see everyone again turned out to be a tour trip where I would only see one cousin, one friend, and a couple old ladies I hardly remember.

First of all, we couldn't get any transportation to where we wanted to go. It seemed like hours waiting at that bus stop. Since there were a lot of buses going to where another aunt lived in St. Ann, Rondah decided to go and get a ride from there. We spent at least two hours at her house before she got a friend that drove a taxi to take us.

Then Rondah broke the news to me. We weren't going to stay very long—we would just say hi and go back with the taxi. Can you believe it? However, we would go straight to a hotel in Ocho Rios where we would stay until the next day and then go to a nearby beach. Anyway, when we got there, memories started rushing back to me. At every house I passed there lingered some memory of something.

We stopped at my old friend Linworth's house. His mother kept saying I've grown a lot. So did Linworth. But he'd grown too. He changed almost completely. His voice changed and he sounds like a man. He asked for my address. I guess we'll keep in touch.

We then went to see my cousin Nicey. She couldn't believe it was me. She told me one of the most disappointing parts of my day—that Janice had moved. I guess I won't be seeing her. Also my old teachers weren't teaching anymore. We didn't even have time to stop at our old house. We only saw it from a hilltop. I really wanted to stay. I still want to go back. The taxi took us to Ocho Rios. At least I had the beach to look forward to. Then what do you know? Devoy gets sick and we have to check out of the hotel after only one hour.

So here I am, back in St. Catherine. I guess this is where I'll be for the whole vacation.

—— ✿ ✿ ✿ ——

April 26, 1991

Dear Janice,

You wouldn't believe how far you have to go to make a phone call in this country. Rondah and I were going to call back home to let everyone know how we are. We had to take a bus just to get to a phone. It's unbelievable. Anyhow, Rondah called. She was on the phone for almost a half hour and no one even asked about me. It was just Devoy, Devoy. I'm not jealous but they could have at least asked how I was doing. It's like they don't care.

My mother wanted us, or at least Rondah and Devoy, to go back at an earlier date when she found out Devoy was sick. By the way, it's just a cold.

We went to the movies with some of Rondah's friends. The movie theaters here are gorgeous and they are huge! At least the one I went to was.

Tomorrow we're going to see a play called 50/50. Everybody is talking about it so I figure it's good. I'll talk to you tomorrow.

April 27, 1991

Dear Janice,

We couldn't get into the play because it was sold out. But it turned out to be a nice day. Rondah, Devoy, Rondah's friend Marcia, our two cousins who we're staying with and myself walked around Kingston and stopped at the shore of some kind of body of water, took pictures, laughed and talked. Kingston I think is the most busy place in Jamaica. It's mostly a business area. There are tall buildings that would be hard to find anywhere else in Jamaica. There are people selling things on the sidewalk and they'll do anything to make you buy from them. They usually travel from poorer areas or farming areas with crops or crafts that they thought people would buy. For most of them, that's their only source of income. It pains me to see people living like that. It's not fair that people suffer while people like Michael Jackson make millions of dollars for singing a song. There's poverty everywhere but at least in New York people can get more help. There is always public assistance like welfare. For the homeless there are shelters. There aren't any things like that in Jamaica. In that case, I'm lucky to be here.

———— ⚭ ⚭ ⚭ ————

April 28, 1991

Dear Janice,

I went to church today with my three cousins. The church wasn't the best church in Jamaica, not even close. I don't know exactly how to describe it. The seats were made out of pieces of board placed down on concrete blocks. The walls had no hint of paint, there were no doors, everything was just thrown together. My cousins tell me it used to look much better but the famous Hurricane Gilbert struck and that was it. They also told me some other stories about Gilbert.

For instance, a lady who lives in their housing scheme's roof was blown off completely and she had to run for shelter at their house. It's a lucky thing that nothing happened to any of my family or their homes. I remember hearing what was happening down here while I was up in New York and praying that nothing would happen to those I loved. That's the worst feeling to have.

April 30, 1991

Dear Janice,

Right now, I'm worried out of my mind. My grand-mother has taken sick and she has to go to the hospital for an operation. I can't believe this is happening to me again. My great grandmother was sick. She had to go to the hospital. She had to take an operation. But she also never came back out. The last time I was with her was when they were putting her in her grave. This cannot happen again. One time was enough for a lifetime.

May 2, 1991

Dear Janice,

Today we went to a place called Glengoff to visit my other set of grandparents. I don't know them very well. They're my father's side. There wasn't anyone home except my father's step-mother. My other grandmother (my father's mother) had died when he was born. She didn't even know who we were until we told her who we were. We showed her Courtney's pictures. She only browsed through and gave them back. She doesn't seem to have a very nice personality.

May 3, 1991

Dear Janice,

Today was pretty boring. In a sense it wasn't though. Because I've been on the road so much, just staying home seems strange it was nice to be with Oudia she's fun. We argue, but it's friendly arguing. There is such a thing! Just last night we were arguing and fist fighting and I told her we're only doing this because we love each other. Is that strange to you? It really isn't. If you were alive with feelings you'd know what I mean. We humans are complicated creatures you know.

May 7, 1991

I'm back home! It's almost like I never left. One thing I've found out about this place is you can leave for weeks or even months and when you get back you get right back into the flow of things. I've only been back a few hours and life has gone back to normal already. Good old Jamaica is behind me now so is the thought that everything had stayed the same after I left. It's kind of nice to know everyone has gone on with their lives down there.

Big news! Sandra has left Dave. She just packed up her things and split. I could sense they were having problems before but it's a shame it ended that way after two years together. He's taking off where I've just left. He's going to Jamaica on Friday. He does need a vacation badly. I'll miss Sandra, he's making her out to be the one at fault. I need to hear both sides though.

I've been calling Derek and I can't reach him. I guess I'll have to wait until tomorrow to talk to him.

My mom's friend is here, she just came in from Jamaica a couple days ago. She'll be here until September and she'll be staying with us! That's six months! She's here working, or at least trying to get a job. I guess there's a lot going on back here. Nothing I can't handle though.

May 8, 1991

Dear Janice,

I skipped school today. I needed a rest from my vacation. Have you ever heard of that? Anyways, I did reach Derek. Actually he called me. He is such a jerk! He was calling from some friends house and even though he had me on the phone, he had his concentration on his stupid friends. But that's o.k., if he doesn't care to hear about my vacation, I won't care to hear about anything he says again. One of the only things he did ask me was if I bought him anything.

May 9, 1991

I want to scream! Going back to school was what I thought it would be unfortunately. It was terrible! I didn't understand the work they were doing and I had to take tests I'd missed. It's amazing the amount of work my class covers in two weeks. I never realized. My homeroom teacher was acting really snotty when he saw me. I had told him before I left where I was going. Still, he acted like I was playing hooky for the past two weeks.

May 11, 1991

Dear Janice,

Dave left for Jamaica today. He's there as I write, right now. It's his first time going back. He was really excited. He probably gets to go around more because he's renting a car. I would have gone all over the place to all the 14 parishes.

I wrote Linworth today. I wrote that I really did want to keep in touch all those years but couldn't. I hope he falls for it. It's true, the part about wanting to but the real reason is I'm lazy. But now is what matters. I really would like to keep in touch.

May 13, 1991

Today I have major bad news. Derek's phone is disconnected. There goes the relationship. I could feel it. I can't call him, he can't call me, we never see each other, so is it over? I've noticed since my return Derek hasn't been calling much and when he does, the conversation is terrible. I imagine now he'll have to use a pay phone. I don't understand this guy. What happened over those two weeks? On the plane, I felt we were so close, now we seemed to have drifted. He claims he missed me, but I just don't know. I think I'm too young for this whole thing. He's way older than me. He won't tell me his right age. I guess he's saying he'll be whatever age I want him to be. Who knows? I just don't know anymore.

May 15, 1991

Dear Janice,

I'm not exaggerating when I talk about how hard it is to get back in the swing of things at school. Math class has been the hardest. It's so hard to keep up with sequential math (the course I'm taking). If you missed one thing, it's hard to understand the other. Maybe I should have waited for summer for my little trip.

May 18, 1991

Dear Janice,

Dave came back. His vacation did do him good. He seems so happy! He was with his old girlfriend Coleen. Apparently they spent a lot of time together because she's all he talks about. They haven't seen each other in 5 years! That's a lot. Anyway, they went all over the place together. He brought back a video with a lot of people from back home on it. Even Derek's dad. Linworth was on it too. I envy him, he did everything he wanted to down there while I did what my sister wanted. It really sucks!

May 21, 1991

Dear Janice,

It's strange to see Dave functioning without Sandra. It's strange to see two people who were so close be like strangers in such a short while. I think that's what'll happen between Derek and me. He's acting too flaky for me lately. He's not the same person he used to be every time we talk. I get so upset when I talk to him because he's like a rock—I can't communicate with him. I knew when his phone cut off that that would be it! If we don't have communication, we have nothing. So I guess right now we have nothing but a few empty phone calls.

May 22, 1991

Dear Janice,

I never updated you on my grandmother. She's recovered from her operation and is doing well. Everyone is really relieved. I'm so happy that I'll continue to have her in my life. I plan to visit her this weekend and give her a big hug and kiss!

May 24, 1991

Dear Janice,

I think I'm settling back down finally in school. It's amazing how only two weeks out of school put me so far behind. I realize how hard it is for people who return to highschool. Now, it seems impossible. I guess I should stick to school so I won't end up going back when I'm old. People should really think before they do something stupid like drop out of school. My mother did when she was 16 and had

Courtney. That was the reason, and she got married at that same age. I take this case to say (and I don't say this often) that my mother was really careless. If she reads this and kills me, I'll regret writing it, but it's true. Maybe that's why she's on my back all the time. She probably doesn't want me to trace her footsteps. I'll try not to—believe me!

May 26, 1991

Dear Janice,

Teniesha and her mom showed up unexpectedly tonight. I hadn't seen her in a really long time. They took me for a ride in her mom's fiance's new car. We stopped off at his workplace. He works at a sort of foster home for boys. When we went in we both thought this guy was really cute. He was sitting by himself on the couch watching t.v. Little did we know the guy was mentally handicapped. The fiance really worked for a home for the mentally handicapped. It goes to show that we think of the handicapped as not being really as important as us. They are people too, no matter what! I learned something today, cuteness goes to everyone. The point is we are not superior to anyone.

May 29, 1991

Dear Janice,

Derek was acting like a real jerk on the phone today. He seemed to be around his friends, and he talked to me like he ruled me or something. He just seemed to be playing a macho role to impress his friends. I hope he doesn't keep this crap up! He's pulling at my last nerve! I really like him, but it's the person he's acting like now that makes me want to curse him out and erase him from my life. I just may do that.

June 2, 1991

Dear Janice,

School is so boring now. There is nothing to do because all the textbooks have been collected and we only have to be present at each class. We could help clean up with the teachers but I'm too lazy for that. It is so funny when you look through the window because kids are just jumping the fence one by one. Some are running through the parking lots.

Anyhow, I did get one assignment today from my Home and Careers teacher. She never quits. Earlier in the year she had made the class write about the goals we have for this, our first year in that school. Today she asked us to write about how it went. Well, to describe my essay I would say I was honest. I didn't hesitate to tell how I felt about all my teachers whether it was good or bad.

What I learned from school was a combination of good and bad. I feel my teachers were excited about their power over students so they focused on that instead of getting through to us. I learned that life is like a garden of roses—roses are pretty to look at and you try to pick one but there'll always be some thorns. School is the same in the sense that a good education that will bring you happiness is like looking at a pretty rose. But in getting to that education, the thorns will be the teachers you don't like, the uninteresting classes, and the kids who want to give you a hard time.

So the good I got from this year is a greater understanding of life. The bad is I had to get pierced by some thorns to reach that understanding.

June 4, 1991

Dear Janice,

My birthday is coming. In nine days I'll be a teenager. My parents are actually looking for an apartment to move—that's the greatest birthday present! I'll miss my friends and everything, but I'll be glad to be out of this place. There's so much about it that is so unattractive. Over the years we've really tried to fix it up but it always looks on the down side. I know wherever we go will be much better than here. I have a lot to look forward to now. I'm finishing school in a couple of weeks and I'm moving in probably the same amount of time. I'm really happy.

June 7, 1991

Dear Janice,

I never considered this before but when we move Rondah won't be coming with us. The plan is that her and Phillip and the baby will be living together. This is a whole lot to take in. I'm going to miss Rondah acting silly around the house and coming home to see Devoy in his crib. It'll only be me and my parents. What a scary thought! When I try to picture it, I see me alone in my room everyday because my mom is at work, and Daddy is sleeping because he has to rest and go to work later. I suppose I'll see Devoy when I babysit but it won't be the same. He will be picked up around 6 because Phillip gets off from work around that time.

I'll miss them so much! I'm glad though that Rondah will have her independence and maybe they'll even get married if living together works out.

June 9, 1991

Dear Janice,

I guess you could say it's over between me and Derek! You can't expect a great explanation because I hardly know how to explain. He's changed so much! A little too much. All of a sudden he says I'm too young to be such a big part of his life. Remember, he never told me his age. Don't take it like he dumped me—I was the one who said, "Don't ever call me again." He really did it! He treated me like dirt. We used to talk like such good friends, now he seems so self-righteous. He acts like he's above everyone else including yours truly.

Well, it's done with now! The worst thing is I came out of it feeling stupid for letting myself like him so much. I shouldn't blame myself though. He was a nice person before. It's maybe his teenage hormones that made him change like this. Whatever it was, him and it should get as far as they can out of this girl's life. He made me feel like dirt and a wish of mine now is that one day I'll be successful and rich and he'll be just the opposite and he'll come running back saying, "Please forgive me." I'll just look at him and laugh and call my butler to personally escort him out!

June 13, 1991

Dear Janice,

Today I am a teenager. I don't know what I'm feeling right now. I'm so happy though. I don't think I've changed since yesterday when I was twelve but it feels good to be a number that ends in teen. I didn't do anything special, I wore a really nice jeans outfit to school that Rondah got me as a present. Everybody is sweating it (meaning, everyone likes it). Rondah always has a present for me on my birthday. My mother and father try to too. But as for Dave and Courtney, they always say to wait until next week. Then when next week comes there is never a present. They're not like that with everyone. They always have something for their girlfriends on their birthdays. This doesn't make me feel that they don't love me, it makes me feel that they don't understand that the thought to buy a present really counts with family. I think they think they've got your love and it really doesn't matter. They have to understand that you have to show it sometimes.

---— ↪ ↪ ↪ —---

June 15, 1991

Dear Janice,

Today I decided to have a little belated birthday party since it's a Saturday and my birthday was this week. We just ordered a cake and got some refreshments. That's not important in this entry though. What is important is that today I found out who my real friends are. I invited all of them, they all said they were coming. I even called up my best friend from last year. Remember the one who moved and went to another school?

Well it turns out that even though she lived the farthest, she was one of the only ones that showed up. I guess this all was short notice, but if all those other girls I call my friends were my friends, they would have made an effort to come.

Isabelle and Denise went to the movies. Their excuse was that they lost their money and had to walk home. They said they had planned to make it though, but by the time they reached home, everything was over. I'll have to tell you more tomorrow.

June 17, 1991

Dear Janice,

I'll have to finish this party story. I don't know where Sandra was, but Deborah was seen walking with another girl, Stacy. They left around 6 and came back around 10. Deborah's excuse is she thought the party would be going on when she came back. I suppose I could have made it go on for longer, but I was too pissed. I just wanted it over.

Well, I had a great time with Teniesha there. We went all around the neighborhood with the other girls there and these two guys, Andrew and Desmond. I'm not really close with the other girls, we just hang out together. I shouldn't have expected so much from them and I'm not going to let them get me down. I'm just glad I found out how good friends they were in the midst of moving.

June 18, 1991

Dear Janice,

They (my mom and daddy) think they've found a place. It's in the Bronx and they say it's really nice. I'll believe it when I see it. But they seem to really think so. They also say it's in a really nice neighborhood. They're going to bring me there on Friday to see it.

At school nobody is really doing anything. The teachers are giving work but kids have just been cutting and going off. It's not like they just walk out, they have to climb the fence in the back. It's really funny. Even girls are doing it.

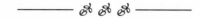

June 19, 1991

Dear Janice,

My parents were right, the apartment is really nice. The neighborhood is spotless and everything looks brand new. There was this little old lady who we are renting it from. She and her husband used to live in there themselves but he's sick in the hospital and she's moving downstairs. She looks really sweet.

Actually, I've fallen in love with this place. It's just right. It's roomy and has a gorgeous interior from the paint to the carpeting. My room is big too. It has a cozy balcony looking over the neighborhood which is full of big, gorgeous houses. It's clean and bright. My parents say I could catch a bus from there to get to school easily. So I guess J.H.S. 80 will see my face again next year. I was kinda hoping that I didn't have to go back. More accurately, I really wanted not to. My parents do because they don't think it's good to change schools a lot. I keep reminding myself that it would have been 3 years if I wasn't in that 2 year program. It helps somewhat to think of that. Well Janice, what can I do? I'm under 18 and under their roof! But I really love the house!

June 20, 1991

Dear Janice,

Here comes very disappointing news. The old lady who's the landlord wasn't as sweet as I made her out to be. She wanted to raise up to rent a little too high. She said her sick husband said it would be best. Anyway, my parents said no and in a way I don't blame them. When they told me, something sunk in my stomach. I'm trying now to think that there are others as good or even better than that one.

One thing is for sure, we're still moving. For that I'm really glad. They're going to start looking again. Meanwhile, Rondah and Phillip are still looking. Everyone is looking for a way out of Bainbridge Ave!

June 21, 1991

Dear Janice,

Today Rondah found her apartment. Again I'm going to see it on Friday. The way she sounds, it's not too hot. Well, if I know Rondah, I know she'll have it looking like a palace in no time at all.

When I told my friends I was leaving everybody except Deborah was really nice about it. They asked me when and how far and everything. Deborah on the other hand was like "Good, I'm not going to miss you!" I would give anything if someone would tell me what her problem is. From the day I met her 5 years ago, she's never had anything nice to say. I think it's just her personality, but I hate it! Deep down, I know she doesn't mean the things she says, but why say them?

June 22, 1991

Dear Janice,

Rondah's apartment doesn't look too pretty. It was really shabby! I pleaded with her not to take it but she claims it has possibilities. As I said before, she could make any place look like a palace. My parents heard about another place in Mt. Vernon. That's not far from the Bronx. It's where Derek lives. I hope I don't run into him if I move there. We'll know next week. They're going to look at it on Monday. That would mean if I move there, a change of schools. Yes!

June 23, 1991

Dear Janice,

I was thinking how after this year of being the little freshman how next year I'll be a senior just like that. Freshmen are going to look up to me! It's such a big change. Tomorrow Deborah is going to graduate. She got into John F. Kennedy High. Next year that will be me graduating. She has her cap and gown all ready. I'm happy for her even though she gets to me sometimes (most times). I won't be seeing her too often next year but I think that will work out for the best. The less I see someone, the more I appreciate them.

June 24, 1991

Dear Janice,

They took the apartment. Mt. Vernon here I come!
Wednesday is the last day of school. We're also
moving on that day—as soon as I get home. The apartment
is definite this time. Everyone likes this new place, they've all
seen it. They say it's very roomy. I am so eager to see it.
Two more days til the last day of school. I'm so glad! I'll
have to say goodbye to everyone and tell them they just
might not see me again. I never made any really close friends
this year. Everyone was just casual acquaintances. I guess I'll
remember this year as the year of casual acquaintances. As
far as things at home, I'll remember it as the year of mom
troubles.

As for the move, I don't know what to say. Where I'm
living now isn't the best place in New York, but it isn't the
worst either. I mean, I look across the street where the guy
from the store was shot and I walk around the corner and
I look at the banner hung in remembrance of George
Gonzalez (he was kidnapped then killed)—he used to live
right there. When I look at those things I'm with no
hesitation ready to go. But then I have to hesitate when I
look at the familiar faces walking up and down the blocks
and I remember block parties. I remember how everyone
pulled together to make them happen every year.

I understand we'll be living in a bigger, nicer house in
a quiet neighborhood. We, is me, and my parents. No

Rondah, no Devoy—that's the biggest blow of it all. I'll see them as often as everyday though because I have to babysit Devoy and but it won't be the same though. I'll be alone in the house, I mean completely alone, with my parents! Oh, man, I can't imagine that. I'm going to miss them both and I know it'll hurt sometimes, but growing up is like a roller coaster, you can only run smooth for a short time and by the time you feel adjusted, there's this big fall. You knew it was coming but when it hits you it's like it wasn't expected.

June 25, 1991

Dear Janice,

You're coming to an end! Tomorrow will be the last day I will write on your pages! My first year of J.H. will be over and after Wednesday, a big part of it will be left behind.

As I said yesterday, I'll remember this year of being a year of casual acquaintances. I didn't get close to anyone outside of my family except Derek. He disappointed me and my heart full one minute, shattered the next. This year has been a not-so-good chapter in the life of myself. Next year I hope it will be one of the better ones. I had so many troubles with my mother. I'm hoping next year we'll smooth it over even though I sincerely doubt it. The older I get, the more harder it gets.

Courtney is married, Dave is single and on his own, I hear

the faint sounds of wedding bells for Rondah and Phillip, I have a nephew; overall a lot has happened that's good. In their lives that is. The only thing for me has been you. This is so much like you're dying. I'll miss you a lot. You know everything that's happened to me since September 10th. I tried never to keep anything back from you but there was always that feeling that someone would be reading your pages not too long from now. I'll miss the idea of you and just everything about this. I'll talk to you tomorrow for the last time. I'll miss you.

June 26, 1991

Dear Janice,

I t's my last day of so much. It's my last day living here on Bainbridge Ave., it's my last day at J.H.S.80, my last day writing to you. In this entry I want to look ahead. I wonder what grade 9 holds for me. I want to look and see how my highschool career will go. I want to settle down and listen to my teachers no matter how hard it is. I'll try to be more open to people and become more of a friend to more people. I'll try not to fall so deep for a guy because I don't want another heartbreak. I'm going to cool it for a while with these thoughts of boys. That is, *if* I can stop. I hope my mother won't be so weird when it comes to them though.

—— ❦ ❦ ❦ ——

The less cautious she is of those things, the less I'll care about them.

All in all, I look for understanding in my future. I just want people to understand me! That would set the pace for the rest of life. With understanding I think I'll achieve anything I want. I just want understanding! Well Janice, this is it. It was fun while it lasted.